A Glance at the Life of the Holy Prophet of Islam

A Glance at the Life of the Holy Prophet of Islam

Dar Rah Haqq's Board of Writers
Translated by N. Tawheedi

A Glance at the Life of the Holy Prophet of Islam

Dar Rah Haqq's Board of Writers
Translated by N. Tawheedi

Jacket Design by: F. Farhang

January 2002

Library of Congress Catalog Card Number: 88-62666
ISBN 0-922817-01-4

January 2002

A glance at the life of the holy prophet of Islam/ Dar Rah Haqq's Board of writers; translated by N. Tawheedi.-- [s. l: s. n], 2002.
151 p.
Cataloging based on CIP information.
Bibliography: p.: 131 - 139.

I.Mohammad. Prophet, d. 632. I.Mo'assese-ye Dar Rah-e Haqq. Hey'at-e Tahririyeh.
II.Towhidi, N.

BP22.9.G530493   297.93
2002
            M78-21069

Contents

Chapter One: The Pre-Islamic World 13
Arabia during the dark pre-Islamic times 14
Chapter Two: The Prophet's Birth and Childhood 19
The wonderful baby 20
Halima, the Prophet's nurse 21
In the storm of events 22
A glimpse into the Prophet's character 22
**Chapter Three: Some Scenes from
the Prophet's Childhood and Youth** 25
A few scenes 25
Bahira's interview with the Prophet 26
The Prophet as a shepherd and a contemplative man 27
The Prophet's chastity 28
Chapter Four: The Prophet's First Marriage 31
Khadija's business proposal 32
Khadija 32
Prophet's journey to Damascus 33
Khadija's proposal of marriage 34
**Chapter Five: The Philosophy of the Marriages
of the Holy Prophet of Islam** 37
*Some examples of the accusations
brought against him by Christians 37*
The judgment of history 38
Groundless views of bigoted critics 39

The number of wives of the Holy Prophet 39
To take care of the orphans and the destitute 40
To establish proper laws and customs 40
False accusations 41
To set free the slaves like Juwayriya 41
To form friendly relations 41

Chapter Six: The Character of the Holy Prophet Before the Actualization of the Prophetic Mission 43

The principle of harmony 43
The environment of Arabia before the advent of Islam 43
Prophets were not products of their environments; they created them 45
The installation of the Black Stone 46

Chapter Seven: The Beginning of the Revelation 49

The Prophet at the age of forty 50
What is revelation? 52
Is revelation a kind of hysteria? 52
Revelation and today's science 53

Chapter Eight: The Prophet's Method of Propagating Islam 55

Khadija waiting for the Prophet 56
'Ali, the first male who came to believe in the Prophet's faith 57
The presentation of ritual prayers as a religious duty 57
Three years of propagation in practice 57
The invitation to his relatives and the first miracle 59

Chapter Nine: The Public Mission of the Prophet of Islam 63

The Prophet's speech on Mount Safa 63
The effect of the speech of the Holy Prophet 64
The Quraysh complain to Abu Talib 65
The Quraysh try to bribe the Holy Prophet 66

Chapter Ten: The Obstacles on the Way and the Tortures Inflicted by the Quraysh 69

Economic struggle 72
Psychological warfare 72

Physical torment and torture 72

Chapter Eleven: The Migration of the Prophet: the Source of Historical Transformation **75**

Going into exile to achieve this divine goal 75
Yathrib — Ready to submit to Islam 76
The plot to murder the Holy Prophet of Islam 76
'Ali's self-sacrifice 77
The Holy Prophet of Islam goes to the Thawr cave 77
On the way to Yathrib 77
Yathrib eagerly awaiting the Holy Prophet 78
A lesson from the Hijra 79

Chapter Twelve: Laying the Foundation for an Islamic Fraternity in Medina **81**

The Prophet's initiative in creating Islamic brotherhood 82
Islamic brotherhood: the byword of unity and fraternity 82
Economic cooperation 83
Scientific and educational cooperation 84
Islamic brotherhood in the present age 84

Chapter Thirteen: Jihad: Religious Struggle and Spiritual Struggle in the Way of God **87**

The purpose of Jihad 88
God's words 89
Did Islam prevail by the force of the sword? 89
Conclusion 90

Chapter Fourteen: The Motives of the Wars of the Prophet **93**

The war of Badr 94
The war of Uhud 95
The Ahzab (Trench) war 96
The Bani Qurayzah war 96
The Bani Mustalaq war 96
The Khaybar war 97
The Mutah war 97
The conquest of Makkah 97
Hunayn and Ta'if 98

Chapter Fifteen: The Universal Mission of the Prophet of Islam:

A Faith for both East and West **101**
Makkah: the starting place for the Prophet's propagation of Islam 103
Another testimony to Islam's universality 103
The letter to Khusrow, the king of Iran 104
To Harqal, the king of Rome 104
A letter to the ruler of Yamamah 105
A letter to the Jews 105
A letter to Bishop Najran 106
Our duty is to convey the message of Islam 106

Chapter Sixteen: Muhammad, the Last Prophet **109**
Comprehensiveness 110
Giving guidance in deadlocks 110
Islam: the immortal faith 111
The end of prophecy with the Prophet 112

Chapter Seventeen: Ghadir and the Prophet's Successor **115**
The narrators of Ghadir 119
The purport of the discourse on Ghadir 120

Chapter Eighteen: The Morals and Behaviour of the Holy Prophet **123**
The Prophet among the people 125
The Prophet's tolerance and forgiveness 127
The Prophet's cleanliness and orderliness 128
The Prophet was a pious and sincere worshipper of God 129

Notes **131**
Index **141**

*In the Name of God
the Merciful, the Compassionate*

Chapter 1

The Pre-Islamic World

Before the advent of Islam, people all over the world were sadly impoverished in thought, opinions, and individual and social attitudes. Although such conditions were not the same in all parts of the world, generally speaking, all the people of the world shared superstitious beliefs, intellectual deviations, inhumane social traditions, myths and social and moral conflicts.

Before Islam emerged, the Jews had changed the religion of Moses into hidebound dogma and its principles into hollow, lifeless rules and precepts. The spirit of materialism had penetrated into people's lives. Unfortunately, Christianity, which had been presented for the moral rectification and spiritual refinement of the people, was changed in nature by the Christian clergy and became a vehicle for the passionate ambitions of most of them. Since it lacked complete, comprehensive laws and regulations for social systems, it proved unable to provide the people with deliverance and comprehensive guidance.

It was due to such conditions that people all over the world shared superstitious ideas, inhuman social traditions, myths, social and moral conflicts.

The fire of corruption and perdition was raging. Superstitions and false views ruled people in the name of religion! Paganism and the concept of the Trinity had been imposed upon them. Many worshipped idols, fire, cows and stars. Most shameful of all was the widespread worship of the sexual organs of men and women.[1] This same moral and spiritual corruption and regression, which had spread everywhere, caused dishonesty, darkness and deviations in human societies. Bloodshed, murder, tyranny, and oppression prevailed all over the world. In fact, humanity had been put on the verge of the abyss of total destruction!

ARABIA DURING THE DARK PRE-ISLAMIC TIMES

Arabia, which has been called 'the burnt land', was then a strange place. A collection of red-hot deserts, valleys, and sand hills was called 'Arabia'. There was hardly any water or plant life in it.

It would have been a mistake to name the people's dwellings 'houses'. They were rather catacombs in which living beings named 'human beings' fidgeted and lived miserably on dates and stinking water! Tribal fights and disputes formed the basic principle of the Arabian social system. Makkah was no more than an idol-temple. Its inhabitants included traders and usurers who even exchanged human life for money.

The people of the Arabian Peninsula suffered from their tribal and pastoral life in the deserts, coupled with blood-thirsty feudalism. The economic crisis resulting from the exploitation of the people by the ruling class and by bands of usurers had robbed human life of its meaning and darkened the horizon of social well-being.

The wealthy usurers who engaged in trade in Makkah had amassed enormous amounts of wealth by illegitimate means and exploited the weak and poor classes of society. In fact, they increasingly exacerbated anti-human social class differences through usury and oppressive exploitation.

Due to their ignorance, the Arab tribes in those days generally engaged in worshipping natural phenomena and in idolatry. The House of God, the Ka'aba, was used as the idol-temple of the Arabs.[2]

Any one of the indecent, degrading social and moral customs in Arabia at that time was enough to destroy the honour of a whole nation. Before Islam, the anti-human deviations of the Arabs had created a situation whereby the fruit was crime and corruption, the nourishment was corpses, the motto was fear and dread, and the logic was the sword.

The Arabs wrongly believed that only those were superior who descended from the Arab race and had Arab blood! As a matter of fact, the twentieth-century form of nationalism and racism was quite prevalent among the Arabs during the first pagan period.[3]

In addition, the Arabs vainly gloried in their wealth and the number of their children. Each tribe having wealth and a large number of offspring prided itself on them and considered them to be among its crowning achievements.

Plunder, robbery, savagery, aggression, and treachery were their obvious characteristics, and genocide was considered a sign of bravery and courage. As the Arabs before the time of Muhammad (peace and the mercy of God be upon him and his descendants) believed the birth of a daughter to be harmful or were either afraid of poverty and destitution, they either killed their innocent daughters or buried them alive. If a man was given the news that his wife had borne a baby daughter, his face would become red with rage. He would then seclude himself plotting what to do with his newborn daughter! Should he bear the shame and disdain and take care of her or should he bury her alive and banish the disgrace and disdain from himself because in some cases even the existence of one daughter in a family was considered shameful.

'And they ascribe daughters to God, glory be to Him, and for themselves (they would have) what they desire. And when a daughter is announced to one of them, his face becomes black and he is full of wrath. He hides himself from the people because of the evil of that which is announced to him. Shall he keep it with disgrace or bury it (alive) in the dust? Now surely evil is what they judge' (16:58-59).

'And do not kill your children for fear of poverty; We give them sustenance and yourselves (too); surely to kill them is a great wrong' (17:31).

In the *Nahj ul-Balaghah*, Imam 'Ali has described the social conditions of the Arabs in the following way, '...And you Arabs were at that time followers of the worst beliefs and lived in a land of burning deserts. You lived on the stony ground amidst poisonous snakes that fled no voice or sounds. You drank polluted water, ate rough, unwholesome foods, shed each other's blood, and removed yourselves from your relatives. Idols had been set all around you and you did not avoid sins...'.[4]

Thus the Arabs lived in a filthy, depraved environment and as a result of misdirection and immaturity, had turned into brutal, plundering, and seditious people. Like most people of that time, they had adopted superstitious, illusive myths, and false notions as 'religion'.[5]

It goes without saying that for a basic reformation of such a society, a fundamental, comprehensive, and all-embracing revolution was quite necessary. However, the leader of such a vital movement and revolution had to be a divine man sent down by God so he would be and would remain devoid of tyranny, and any aggressive, selfish tendencies, and would not destroy his enemies for his own selfish interests, under the pretext of purification, but would try to reform and rectify them, working solely for God's sake, for the people's welfare, and for the improvement of human societies.

There is no doubt that a leader who is himself immoral, unscrupulous, and without praise-worthy human characteristics is unable to rectify human societies and save the people. It is only divine leaders who, inspired by Almighty God, are able to make profound basic transformations in all phases of the people's individual and social life.

Now we must try to understand what kind of person such a leader of the worldwide revolution was and what changes he made in the world.

Chapter 2

The Prophet's Birth and Childhood

Makkah was covered by a heavy blanket of darkness. No signs of life and activity could be observed in it. Only the moon slowly emerged from behind the darkened surrounding mountains and cast its pale, delicate rays upon the simple, austere houses and upon the sandy regions outside the city.

Little by little, midnight gave way to dawn. A gentle breeze rustled through the burning land of the Hijaz and prepared it for a short rest. Now the stars, too, added to the beauty of this pure banquet of nature and smiled at the residents of Makkah.

It was now early dawn and the early rising, vigilant night birds were singing beautifully in that heavenly weather. They seemed to be speaking in a romantic language to their Beloved! The horizon was on the verge of the brightness of dawn but still a mysterious silence prevailed over the city. All were asleep. Only Amina was awake, feeling the contractions she had been expecting.

Gradually the contractions became stronger. Suddenly Amina saw several unknown women in her room. The room was filled with light and there was fragrance in the air. She wondered who they were and how they had entered her room through the closed door.[6]

Soon her baby was born, and thus, after several months of waiting, Amina had the pleasure of seeing her child in the early dawn of the 17th of Rabi ul-Awwal.[7]

All were overjoyed with the child's birth. But when Muhammad (peace and the mercy of God be upon him and his descendants) illuminated Amina's dark and silent room of prayer, her young Abdullah, was not present. He had passed away in Medina while returning from Damascus and had been buried there, leaving Amina alone.[8]

THE WONDERFUL BABY

The Prophet was born and his blessed birth gave rise to numerous wonderful incidents in the sky and on the earth, especially in the East, the cradle of civilization.

News of these events spread quickly and informed the people of an imminent, very significant incident. Since this newborn child was predestined to destroy the people's old superstitious beliefs and customs and to lay new foundations for human progress and prosperity, from the very beginning he sounded the reveille.

On that blessed night, the Persian monarch Anushiravan's magnificent palace, which incarnated a false fantasy of power and eternal monarchy and upon which people looked with fear and awe, trembled.[9] Fourteen of its turrets collapsed, and the fire in the fire-temple of Persia, which had been flaming for 1,000 years, was suddenly extinguished.[10]

So the humiliated worshippers of that false, destructive object of worship, whose minds had been blocked by the obstacles of prejudice and false imitation and who thus could not reflect upon nature took notice of the truth and were attracted toward a totally different direction. The drying out of the Savah Lake awakened the people of another great region.[11]

HALIMA, THE PROPHET'S NURSE

For many centuries it had been customary among the Arabs to give their newborn children to women from the tribes around the city to be wet-nursed. This was done so that their children would grow up in the fresh air and the natural environment of the desert and also learn the eloquent Arabic dialect whose purest form was to be found at that time in the desert.[12]

For this reason and since Amina had no milk to feed her child, Abdul Muttalib, his grandfather and guardian, felt it necessary to employ an honorable, trustworthy lady to look after the child of his dear son, Abdullah. After making appropriate inquiries, he selected Halima, who was from the Bani Sa'd tribe (a tribe famous for bravery and eloquence) and who was rated among the most chaste, noble women.

Halima took the infant to her own tribe and looked after him as though he were her own child. The Bani Sa'd tribe had long been suffering from famine in the desert. The dry desert and lack of rains had added much to their poverty and misery.

But from the very day he entered Halima's house, good fortune and blessings entered with him. Her life, which had been filled with poverty and destitution, suddenly changed into a happy and prosperous one. The pale faces of Halima and her children became rosy and full of life. Her dry breasts swelled with milk, and the pasture of the sheep and camels of that region turned fresh and green, whereas before he came to their tribe, people lived in poverty and faced many difficulties.

He grew up more rapidly than other children, ran more nimbly, and did not stammer like them. Good fortune and auspiciousness so accompanied him that all the people around him easily realized this fact and admitted it. Halima's husband, Harith, told her, 'Do you know what a blessed baby we have been given?'[13]

IN THE STORM OF EVENTS

The Prophet was just six years old[14] when his mother, Amina, left Makkah for Medina to visit her relatives and probably to pay a respectful visit to her husband's grave. He accompanied his mother on that trip. But after visiting her relatives and expressing love and loyalty to her husband at Abdullah's graveside, on her way back to Makkah, Amina passed away at a place named Abwa'.[15] Thus, the Prophet had lost both his mother and father by that tender age when every child needs a father's affections and a mother's loving embrace.

A GLIMPSE INTO THE PROPHET'S CHARACTER

Just as the Prophet's birth and the events that followed his blessed birth were extraordinary and suggestive of his majesty and supreme character, so his behaviour and manner of speaking in childhood also made him different from other children. Abdul Muttalib realized this fact and respected his majesty greatly.[16]

Abu Talib, the Prophet's uncle, used to say, 'We have never heard any lies from Muhammad, nor have we seen him misconduct himself or make mischief. He never laughs unduly nor speaks idly and he is mostly alone'.[17]

The Prophet was seven years old when the Jews remarked, 'In our Books we have read that the Prophet of Islam refrains from eating any food which is religiously prohibited or doubtful. Let's try him'.

So they stole a hen and sent it to Abu Talib. Not knowing that the hen had been stolen, all ate from the cooked hen but Muhammad, who avoided even tasting it. When they asked the reason for this avoidance of the food, he answered, 'This food is forbidden by God, and God protects me against anything that He has forbidden...'.

Then the Jews took a hen from a neighbour, intending to pay for it later on, and sent it to Abu Talib's house. Again he avoided eating the hen, saying, 'This food is doubtful and...'.

Then the Jews said, 'This child has an extraordinary character and a supreme position'.[18]

Abdul Muttalib, the chief of the Quraysh tribe, did not treat his grandson like other children, but held him in great respect and reverence.

When a special place was arranged for Abdul Muttalib at the Ka'aba, his offspring surrounded that special place, inhibited by Abdul Muttalib's dignity and glory from stepping into his abode. But the Prophet was by no means impressed by so much grandeur and honour and would always directly go to that particular seat. Abdul Muttalib's sons tried to hinder him, but he protested and said, 'Let my son go. I swear by God that he has a glorified, majestic position'.

Then Muhammad sat beside the chief of the Quraysh, Abdul Muttalib, and spoke with him.[19]

Chapter 3

Some scenes from the Prophet's childhood and youth

A FEW SCENES
Muhammad went through the difficulties of orphanhood in his childhood with the support of his high-spirited grandfather, Abdul Muttalib, and his affectionate uncle, Abu Talib. It seems that the heart-rendering pains of orphanhood must have severely tormented his pure delicate soul. It is logical to believe that these sufferings were necessary for the foundation of his supreme character and that such difficulties taught him how to resist the hardships of life and to bear the heavy responsibility later to be put on his blessed shoulders.

As time went on, Muhammad grew up and his childhood gave place to youth, when instincts and potentials bloom. Although he was deprived of a mother's care and a father's affection, he received affectionate care and attention from Abu Talib, who, due to his moral attitudes and in obedience to his father's emphatic order, protected and supported him. In fact, Muhammad represented three things to Abu Talib: a son, a reminder of his brother, Abdullah, and of his father, Abdul Muttalib. So the Prophet became a beloved member of Abu Talib's family, lived in his house, and was treated as his own son. To the Prophet, Abu Talib was an affectionate father, a loyal uncle, and a compassionate preceptor. These two — uncle and nephew — were so fond of each other that their lives seemed to be intertwined. This very intense affection had caused Abu Talib to refuse to ever part from him. He would take his hand in his own and go with him to the famous Arab markets of 'Akaz, Majnah, and Zil-Majaz. Even when he was to accompany the caravan on travelling on business from Makkah to Damascus, he could not bring himself to part with his nephew. So Abu Talib took him along to Damascus. Riding on a camel, the Prophet started the long journey to Yathrib and Damascus.[20]

BAHIRA'S INTERVIEW WITH THE PROPHET

On the day the Quraysh caravan was nearing Basra,[21] Bahira, a devout monk, caught sight of it through his monastry's window. He observed the caravan shaded by a little cloud that kept pace with it.

Bahira came out of his monastry, stood in a corner and instructed his servant, 'Go and tell them that today they are all my guests'.

All came to him but the Prophet, who was standing beside the property and equipment of the caravan. Seeing that the cloud had ceased to move, Bahira asked his guests, 'Are all the members of the caravan present here?' They answered, 'All but a youth who is the youngest'. Bahira said, 'Tell him to come as well'. So he was asked to come to the monk's room. The keen eyes of Bahira noticed that the cloud over his head moved with him. Taken by surprise, Bahira kept staring at the young boy. When the meal was over, the pious monk told him, 'I have a question to ask you and you must swear by Lat and 'Uzza[22] to answer my question'.

Muhammad said, 'These two you have asked me to swear by are the most detestable things to me'. Bahira said, 'Swear by Allah to answer my question'.

He said, 'Ask your question'.

After a short interview with him, Bahira knelt down before him and started kissing his hands and feet, saying, 'If I live till you start your divine mission, I will most faithfully aid you and fight your enemies. You are superior to all of Adam's offspring...'.

Then he asked, 'Whose son is this youth?' The caravan members pointed to Abu Talib, saying, 'His son'. Bahira said, 'No. His father must be dead!'

Abu Talib said, 'You are right. He is my nephew'. Bahira then said, 'This youth will have a brilliant, extraordinary future. If the Jews find out what I have realized about him, they will destroy him. Take great care lest the Jews should hurt him'.

Abu Talib said, 'What is he destined to do? What have the Jews to do with him?' Bahira said, 'He is predestined to become a Prophet, and the angel of inspiration will come down and make divine revelations to him'. Abu Talib said, 'God will not leave him alone and will Himself protect him against the Jews and his malevolent enemies'.

THE PROPHET AS A SHEPHERD AND A CONTEMPLATIVE MAN

Although Abu Talib was rated as a man of status among the Quraysh, his income was not sufficient to support his family. Now that Muhammad was of mature age, he was naturally inclined to find a job to ease the heavy burden upon his uncle's shoulders. But what kind of job should he engage in to suit his supreme character?

Since he was destined to become a great Prophet and a sublime leader, to face unrestrained obstinate people, to fight against the superstitious beliefs and wrong customs of the period of ignorance, and to lay the foundations of the magnificent palace of justice and proper laws and regulations, he found it expedient to become a herdsman.

Our Holy Prophet would take the sheep and cattle of his relatives and those of the people of Makkah to the surrounding deserts to graze. He gave his uncle the wages he received in return.[24]

This engagement outside the noisy, agitated environment of the city and away from people's disputes and conflicts gave him an invaluable opportunity to acquire much experience, of which the sweet fruits appeared during his prophethood and time of leadership.

Indeed, during this period, he acquired many superior human characteristics such as generosity, good temper, magnanimity, good behaviour towards neighbours, tolerance, truthfulness, trustworthiness, and avoidance of vices. He became known as 'Muhammad, the Trustworthy'.[25]

THE PROPHET'S CHASTITY

When childhood gives its place to maturity and human instincts and potentialities bloom, youngsters suddenly find themselves in the stormy stage of maturity — much more exciting and agitating than childhood. During this critical period of life, various kinds of deviations, seditions, moral deteriorations, and forms of heedlessness threaten the young and their future life. Unless they are properly directed and carefully looked after, or themselves endeavour to control and restrain their overflowing instincts, they will so fall into the terrible abyss of misery and immorality that they can hardly attain happiness and prosperity for the rest of their lives.

The Prophet lived in a severely polluted environment, the atmosphere of which was darkened with all kinds of moral deteriorations and sins. In the Hijaz, not only the youth, but also the aged had become most shamefully involved in sexual deviations and unchasity. In every alley and neighbourhood, black flags had been hung over some houses as a sign of corruption, inviting unvirtuous people inside.

The Prophet grew up in such a foul society, but though he remained unmarried until the age of 25, the sordid environment could not affect him the least bit, nor did anybody observe any immoral action springing from him. Both his friends and his enemies regarded him as the best model of chastity and virtue.

The poems commemorating his blessed marriage with Khadija — the great lady of the Quraysh — remind us of his modesty. Addressing Khadija, the poet says, '...O Khadija, among all the people of the world, you have attained a sublime position, the most honourable position. You have been granted the honour of being wife to Muhammad, the great man whose peer has not been born by any woman in the whole world. All praiseworthy virtues and majestic qualities plus modesty are to be found in him and will be so forever'.[26]

Another poet had said, 'If Ahmad is weighed against all other creatures, he will outweigh them, and truly his virtues are obvious to the Quraysh'.[27]

Chapter 4

The Prophet's First Marriage

Youth is the period of the blooming of instincts and the emergence of one's sexual potencies. When youngsters, both male and female, are of mature age, they are drawn to the opposite sex, and a fire of passion starts flaming in their hearts that will not be extinguished unless they form a union of marriage. It is only in this way that they will find peace of mind.

Therefore, to make the proper use of such potentials and to prevent the various deviations that overflowing sexual instincts may create in human societies, Islam has emphatically ordered that the youth should marry as soon as possible and not shun the command of marriage on the pretext that they may be unable to support their family later on.

'And marry those among you who are single and those who are fit among your male slaves and your female slaves; if they are needy, God will make them free from want out of His grace; and God is

Most Generous, Knowing. And let those who do not find the means to marry keep chaste until God makes them free from want out of His grace' (4:31-32).

But there may be times when financial conditions do not permit one to undertake the responsibilities of married life. No doubt, under such circumstances, marriage must be postponed until conditions are favourable, and, all through this period of celibacy, the youth must necessarily acquire virtue and chastity.

Muhammad suffered just such hard conditions. Due to financial problems, he was unable to take a wife until he was 25.[28] So he found it advisable to temporarily refrain from marriage and to wait for a suitable occasion when life's conditions would allow the formation of a family.[29]

KHADIJA'S BUSINESS PROPOSAL

Khadija, who was an honourable wealthy woman, used to put her wealth at the disposal of others who traded for her and received wages in return for their services.

As Muhammad's fame for honesty, virtue and trustworthiness spread throughout Arabia and reached Khadija, she started seeking his cooperation. Then she made this proposal to him: 'I will put at your disposal some property plus a servant, Masara, and pay you more than others'.

Being well aware of his uncle's financial problems due to his old age, low income, and large family, Muhammad accepted Khadija's offer.[30]

KHADIJA

Khadija, the daughter of Khuwalid, was a lady of supreme character. She had been twice married, to Abu Halah and Atigh Makhzumi, and twice widowed. Though she was forty years old, her enormous wealth, popularity, and prestige had led many wealthy and powerful Quraysh to court her.

But she did not accept any of them as her husband and avoided marriage, for she knew well that they either were interested in her wealth or were men whose character she detested.[31]

PROPHET'S JOURNEY TO DAMASCUS

When the commercial caravan of the Quraysh was ready to start moving towards Damascus and the Prophet, too, had made provisions for the trip and was about to join the caravan, Khadija ordered her servant, Masara, to accompany him to Damascus and be always ready to serve him.

Obviously, it is not possible to explain in detail this historical journey, and we content ourselves with mentioning the following points: This journey brought about many blessings and much good fortune, such as enormous profits in commerce, the manifestation of the Prophet's wonderful personality to the people in the caravan, the meeting with the Christian monk, the prediction of his prophecy,[32] and the preliminary causes of an auspicious matrimonial union. When the trading was over, the caravan returned from Damascus.

Masara explained the trip to Khadija in detail, reporting the huge, unprecedented profits they had gained. She also spoke about the Prophet's excellent character and his generosity, as well as his many other virtues manifested during this journey.[33]

Upon hearing this and hearing about the predictions of a learned Jewish man about his divine character and his marriage with the most honorable woman of the Quraysh, Khadija not only started to cherish his love in her pure heart, but also came to realize that he was her ideal husband.[34]

Also, her uncle, Warqa ibn Nawfal, had talked to her about the predictions of the last prophets, and about the good news of his marriage with Khadija.[35] These words, too, added to her love and enthusiasm.

But how was she to talk to him about her desire and heavenly affection? This was not so easy for Khadija, who was herself the most respected woman of the Quraysh.

KHADIJA'S PROPOSAL OF MARRIAGE

Khadija asked Nafisa, who was her close friend and whom she always trusted with her secrets, to speak to the Prophet about marriage. Nafisa went to him and asked, 'Why do you not get married?' He answered, 'My living conditions and financial situation do not allow me to get married'. Nafisa said, 'Will you agree to get married if this problem is solved and a rich, beautiful, and honorable woman from a well-known family asks you to marry her?'

He asked, 'Who is this woman you are talking about?' Nafisa answered, 'Khadija'.

He said, 'How is it possible? She has rejected the proposals of many of the Quraysh aristocrats and rich men. Would she marry me?' Nafisa said, 'This union is possible and I will arrange it'.

When he became quite sure of Khadija's inclination towards marriage with him, the Prophet talked to his uncles about the matter. They were very pleased with this good news, and they attempted to arrange the marriage for their blessed nephew. And finally this auspicious marriage was celebrated with special ceremonies.[37]

The Prophet spent 25 years of his life with Khadija, who was not only a loving wife for him, but also his best and most helpful mate.[38] This period is considered to be the best period of his married life.

Khadija, peace be upon her, was the first woman who believed in the Prophet's divine prophecy. She put all her wealth at his disposal to propagate and promote Islam.[39] Six children were born of his marriage: two sons named Qasim and Tahir who passed away as infants in Makkah and four daughers named Ruqiyah, Zaynab, Umm Kulsum, and Fatima, who was the most prominent and honoured of them all.[40]

Khadija was so devoted to her husband and showed such great

sympathy and self-sacrifice for him and for the promotion of his religion that not only did he love her dearly and respect her highly during her lifetime, but even after her death. Each time he remembered her, his blessed heart filled with sorrow[41] and he wept at her loss. Khadija's brilliant sun of life set at the age of 65, ten years after the actualization of the prophetic mission of the Prophet.[42] In this way, the house of our Holy Prophet became deprived of the light of Khadija's existence forever.

Chapter 5

The Philosophy of the Marriages of the Holy Prophet of Islam

SOME EXAMPLES OF THE ACCUSATIONS BROUGHT AGAINST HIM BY CHRISTIANS

At the beginning of the 18th century, Christian writers began a new crusade against Islam. Through writing and circulating books over-flowing with insults and false accusations, they intended to distract the people of the world from the divine religion of Islam and to turn them against the great leader of Islam, Prophet Muhammad (peace and the mercy of God be upon him and his descendants).[43]

These myths, false writings, and prejudiced works of the Christian bigots originated in the Middle Ages, especially in the 15th century, when one John Andre Maure wrote a book against the Prophet's religion that was used by the later anti-Islamic writers. And since other writers did not know the Arabic language, they contented themselves with copying out of his books on Islam.[44]

Thus, the writers whose so-called sacred books openly accuse prophets[45] of adultery have written about our great leader, 'He followed passions and sensual desires and though he ordered his followers not to take more than four permanent wives, he himself had more wives'.[46]

With this insult, they have tried to introduce our Holy Prophet as a sensual man to the unaware Christian readers, thus to stain his supreme character and to hinder the spread and propagation of Islam.

But this fantasy turned out to be vain. Before long, the honest Christian writers began to defend the Holy Prophet of Islam and to apologize for the accusations brought against the Qur'an and the Prophet of Islam.

It is clear to those of us who believe in the perfect innocence of prophets, that such insults are quite unbelievable and far from the truth, but it is necessary to make the facts clear to those who do not agree with us in this matter.

THE JUDGMENT OF HISTORY

It has been written by impartial truth-seeking historians, both Muslims and Christians, that the numerous marriages of the Holy Prophet of Islam, were by no means due to sensuality and sexual passions, for if this were so, he would never have married Khadija who was 40 years old and who had lost most of her beauty and vivacity in the houses of her two former husbands, when he himself was only 25, the age of the sexual passions of youth and when young men are preoccupied with choosing young wives.

The Prophet lived most sincerely and faithfully for 25 years with Khadija[47], and, though many beautiful Arab maidens and women were eagerly longing to marry him, not once did he take another wife during his married life with Khadija. No doubt if our Holy Prophet were interested in following sexual passions, he could not have refrained from mating with young women during this long period.

GROUNDLESS VIEWS OF BIGOTED CRITICS

What if such unjust people were asked, 'Why did the Prophet spend his youth with an aged widow and not marry other women? Why did he take several women as wives in the last ten years of his life, which was the period of old age and when he was having to handle many problems regarding both the internal and external policies of Islam, it was not convenient for him to undertake the responsibilities of marital life?'

And what if they were asked, 'Was it not extremely troublesome and difficult to take care of helpless women each having several orphans? Is it consistent with the pleasure-seeking nature of a man to bear the companionship of women with varied moods and manners?'

Surely they have no choice but to admit that the Prophet was never sensual and pleasure-seeking and that they have accused him out of hostility and bigotry.

John Davenport says, 'How is it possible for a sensual man to content himself with just one wife for 25 years in such a place where polygyny was common and prevalent.[28]

THE NUMBER OF WIVES OF THE HOLY PROPHET

After Khadija passed away, when the Holy Prophet was 53 years old, he took other wives including 'Aisha, Hafsa, Zaynab bint Khuzayma, Umm Salma, Sauda bint Zama, Zaynab bint Jahash, Juwayriya, Safia, Maymuna, Umm Habiba and Marya.[49]

The conditions and circumstances that necessitated the several marriages of the Prophet should be studied. The main reasons for his marriages are the following:

1. To take care of the orphans and the destitute

The Prophet took some of his wives in order to maintain the prestige and reputation they had when they previously had been living in comfort and honour but whose faith and honour were endangered due to the loss of their guardians — husbands, fathers, sons and their tribes — forcing them to abandon Islam and select polytheism and atheism. Sauda was like this. Her husband passed away in Ethiopia, where they had migrated, leaving her alone and without support. The Prophet, who had lost Khadija and had no other wife, married Sauda.[50]

Zaynab the daughter of Khuzayma was a widow who had, after her husband's death, fallen into poverty. She had always been a generous and benevolent woman, known as 'the mother of the poor'. To guard her honour and reputation, the Prophet took Zaynab as his wife. She passed away in the lifetime of God's Messenger.[51] Umm Salma, too, was faithful and aged and had helpless orphans. She was another wife of our Prophet.[52]

2. To establish proper laws and customs

Another reason was to establish proper laws and customs and to nullify wrong customs and beliefs of the period of ignorance and idol-worship. At the Holy Prophet's order, Zaynab, the daughter of Jahash and the Prophet's cousin, married Zayd ibn Harith. This was an example of annuling class differences which Islam forbids. Zaynab was a granddaugher of the Quraysh chieftain Abdul Muttalib and Zayd's family were slaves. The Holy Prophet had bought his freedom. For these reasons, Zaynab considered herself superior to her husband, Zayd, thus making her marital life bitter and unbearable. No matter how much the Holy Prophet advised them, she did not change her manners, so finally Zayd, feeling no love for her any longer, divorced her.[53]

At God's command, the great Prophet of Islam married Zaynab after her husband, Zayd, had divorced her in order to wipe out the custom of not marrying the former wives of adopted sons (for they regarded their adopted sons as their real sons), which custom was unduly prevalent among the people in the dark periods of paganism.[54]

False Accusations

Some Christian writers have, in their dishonest judgments and accusatory remarks, gone so far as to claim that the Holy Prophet of Islam had fallen in love with Zaynab's beauty. This claim is so far from the truth that it is clearly rejected by all authentic histories and logical indictions because if the Prophet of Islam were a slave to his passions and entangled in such sensual thoughts, or if Zaynab were so attractive as to fascinate him, he would have fallen in love with her when she was still a maiden, when he himself was young and more vivacious, especially considering the fact that Zaynab was a close relative of his and usually relatives know about each other's beauty or lack of it.

3. To set free the slaves like Juwayriya

Juwayriya was from the famous tribe called the Bani Mustalaq who were defeated and taken captive in their fight with the Islamic forces. The Prophet married Jawayriya the daughter of Harith, who was their chief. When the Muslims observed that the captives had thus become relatives of the Prophet, they freed many of them. According to Ibn Hisham, this blessed marriage resulted in freedom for one hundred families from that tribe.[55]

4. To form friendly relations

Some marriages occurred to form friendly relations with great Arab tribes, to hinder their obstruction, and to maintain internal policy. For these reasons, the Holy Prophet of Islam married 'Aisha, Hafsa, Safia, Maymuna, and Umm Habiba.

Umm Habiba was the daughter of Abu Sufyan, whose family members were bigoted enemies of the family of the Holy Prophet of Islam and especially of our Prophet himself. Umm Habiba's husband gave up Islam in Ethiopia, became a Christian, and died there. She was then extremely troubled and worried for she was herself a Muslim while her father, Abu

Sufyan, was rated among the greatest enemies of Islam. Thus she could not take refuge with him and was alone and helpless. Therefore, to help and support this poor woman and to make friends with the Bani Ummayad, the Prophet married her.[56]

Safia was the daughter of Hayy ibn Akhtab, the head of the Bani Nazir tribe. To guard her prestige, the Prophet took her as his wife after the Jewish captives were scattered among the Muslims, thus establishing family relationships with one of the greatest Bani Israel tribes.[57]

Maymuna, whom God's Messenger married in the year 7 AH, was from the tribe of Bani Makhzum.[58] With the exception of 'Aisha, most of the wives of the Holy Prophet were either widows or divorcees at the time they were married to the Prophet and most of them had lost their beauty and youth, proving that the marriages of the Holy Prophet had been out of sacred motives and for benevolent reasons, so that no one can bring such accusations as sensuality and seeking of false pleasure against him.

Chapter 6

The Character of the Holy Prophet before the actualization of the prophetic mission

THE PRINCIPLE OF HARMONY
Psychologists believe that the environment lays the foundations of people's character and their way of thinking and that the principle of harmony causes the people to follow the society's dominant patterns of thought and behaviour.[59]

Although some of these psychologists have gone to extremes in this matter and have regarded this theory as a general and all-embracing principle, according to which all social phenomena without exception may be analyzed, the principle of the effect of the society on people's morale is undeniable.

Therefore, an environment of virtue and health produces pious and normal offspring, and a corrupt, deviated society will naturally lead people into the pit of corruption and deviation.

Thus, those who remain untouched by the society's deviating factors, must be exceptional people.

THE ENVIRONMENT OF ARABIA BEFORE THE ADVENT OF ISLAM

At that time, the whole world, especially Arabia, was steeped in ignorance, corruption, and turmoil. The Arabs were suffering immensely from superstitions and unchasteness. Ignorance had darkened the lives of the Arabs, who were leading tormented lives. Plunder and murder were quite prevalent — plunder of the people's meager properties and unjust killing!

Most shameful of all was their worship of lifeless statues — idols.[60] False beliefs and class differences were strong. What was lacking was law and justice. The apathetic, wealthy people amassed wealth by exploiting the weak and by overcharging the orphan and the widow. They lorded over the poor class and exploited them.

Their manners in business were so illogical and unjust that they would hold women responsible for their husbands' debts and would detain the husbands for the indebtedness of their poor wives.[61]

Instead of acquiring knowledge and virtue, they prided themselves in their ancestors and in the large numbers of their relatives; sometimes they even went to cemeteries[62] and counted the number of their dead relatives to prove there were more people in their tribe than in other tribes.

Murder, bloodshed, drinking, and illegitimate sexual intercourse were quite ordinary and commonplace.[63] Amr ul-Qays, the famous Arab poet, discussed his satanic sexual relationships with his cousin 'Anizah. Curiously, such poems were ranked among the greatest works of literature and were hung in the Ka'aba.[64]

Such was the situation and moral conditions of a miserable society out of whose dark horizon came the light of Islam.

It is crystal clear that a person who not only is not affected by such a corrosive society, but also grieves over it and attempts to combat it, possesses a great divine character and is competent to lead people and guide them onto the path of salvation.

PROPHETS WERE NOT PRODUCTS OF THEIR ENVIRONMENTS: THEY CREATED THEM

All went to the idol-temples except the Prophet who, without being taught by anybody, made his way to Mount Hira, the mountain where he devotedly worshipped the Creator of the universe and praised His glory and power.[65]

'And you did not recite before it any book, nor did you transcribe one with your right hand, for then could those who say untrue things have doubted' (29:48).

Favoured by Almighty God, he distinguished his path from the very beginning, denounced the wrong manners of his people without any hesitation or fear, and proceeded against those wrong deeds and beliefs.[66]

Not only was not one single moment of his blessed life spent in idolatry, but, as we have already mentioned, he hated to hear the names of idols.[67]

His chasteness and purity were known to all. His extreme honesty led the people to give him the title of 'the Trustworthy', and this great virtue led Khadija to trust him with her commercial property.

The behaviour of the Prophet toward the people and his manners were so pleasant and excellent that they attracted all people. 'Ammar said, 'The Prophet and I were engaged as shepherds before the advent of the prophetic mission. One day I suggested to him, 'Let's go to the Fakh pasturage'. He agreed.

'The next day I went there and saw that he had preceded me but prevented his sheep from grazing there. I asked him the reason. He replied, 'I did not wish my sheep to graze here before your sheep because we had taken this decision together'.[68]

Thus the Prophet took a different direction than his people and was by no means infatuated with tribal customs and moods. In reality, under the control of the divine power, he advanced on his path of evolution and perfection.

For all these reasons, people had great respect for him and relied heavily on his views in solving their problems.

THE INSTALLATION OF THE BLACK STONE

When the Holy Prophet was 30 years old, the Quraysh decided to repair the House of God, the Ka'aba, and since all the tribes of the Quraysh wished to have the honour of this great task, each took on the task of repairing one part of the House of God.

First Walid started to demolish the House and then the others helped him until the pillars that the Prophet Abraham (peace be upon him) had laid down, appeared. Now it was the time for the reconstruction of the Holy House, and each tribe undertook one part of it. When the process of construction reached the point where the Black Stone was to be installed, severe disputes arose among the Quraysh tribes. All of them wanted to have the honour of completing the task.

Little by little, the dispute turned into harsh enmity, and the various tribes got ready for a bloody war. The sons of Abdul Dar filled a large jar with blood and put their hands into it, thereby giving each other a pledge of death at the battlefield.

This terrible discord went on for four or five days until Abu Amayah, who was the oldest of the Quraysh, said, 'My proposal is that we select the first person who enters the mosque as an arbiter and that all of us accept his view on the problem so it will be solved'.

The Quraysh accepted his proposal and waited to see who would enter the mosque first. Suddenly the Holy Prophet of Islam came in. As soon as the people caught sight of him, they said, 'This is the Trustworthy one. This is Muhammad. We will accept his decision'.

The Prophet did not know about the matter. When they explained their problem to him, he said, 'Bring me a piece of cloth'. Although the Quraysh did not know what he meant by that order, they brought the cloth immediately. The Holy Prophet spread the cloth, put the Black Stone in the middle of it, and said, 'Each tribe should take hold of one side of the cloth so all can share in the honour'. The Quraysh did as he had told them and lifted the Black Stone to the point where it was to be installed. Then the Holy Prophet, who observed that if he let any of them install it, conflict and disputes would arise, himself lifted the Black Stone and installed it in its place. Through this excellent device, he put an end to the terrible enmity and conflicts.[69]

This incident clearly demonstrates the supreme character of the Holy Prophet of Islam and his excellent thought and intelligence, which ended a serious dispute without any bloodshed.

Chapter 7

The Beginning of the Revelation

We have so far taken a glance at the earlier part of the blessed life of the Holy Prophet of Islam. Now we must talk about some of the most momentous phases of his life. By the age of 40 he was still living among an extremely backward people who were devoid of any traces of civilization and humanity. These hard conditions severely tormented his pure soul. He observed nothing in that society but the darkness of ignorance. He would go to the Ka'aba, but instead of witnessing the worship of God, he witnessed idolatry. He would then leave the Ka'aba and go among the people. But there, too, he was troubled by what he saw. He was pained by the ugly customs and false thoughts of his people. The pitiable condition of the poor and the destitute caused him great anguish. The deplorable situation of women, who were treated worse than animals, as well as the prevalence of gambling, wine drinking and murder tortured his blessed heart.

When he dealt with people as a merchant, their immoral

behaviour gave so severe an emotional shock to him that he had to go to a lonely place where he would not be tormented by people's inhuman behaviour. For these reasons and to find peace of mind, he would go to Mount Hira and there think deeply about the amazing phenomena of nature and the vestiges of God's All-Embracing Compassion.[70]

THE PROPHET AT THE AGE OF FORTY

By the time the Holy Prophet of Islam reached the age of 40, he was ready for his divine mission.[71] One day suddenly, while he sat in a cave at Mount Hira, Gabriel, the Angel of Revelation, appeared to him and said, 'Recite!' He said in surprise, 'What shall I recite?' Again the divine voice very clearly and openly called out, 'Recite, O Muhammad!'

And a third time Gabriel repeated,[72] *'Recite in the Name of Your Lord Who created. He created the human being from a clot. Recite and your Lord is Most Honourable, Who taught (to write) with the pen, taught the human being what he knew not'* (95:1-5).

An indescribable excitement and eagerness overcame the Holy Prophet, for he had come into contact with a supreme supernatural world. His high spirit had now found a sacred support and an eternal refuge. He saw in himself the power of prophecy. No longer was any worry or agitation to be found in his blessed being. There was now just peace and confidence within him.

Was the Prophet really going through the learning process in that cave on Mount Hira? Some orientalists and foreign authors have answered this question in the affirmative. They have remarked, 'On Mount Hira, the Prophet thought deeply about the concepts of the Bible as well as the instructions of the prophets. There he spent his time in meditation and enjoyed this intellectual meditation'.[73]

This remark is meant to imply that he was a self-made man who invented the religion of Islam by studying and carefully thinking about the Old and New Testaments! But there are certain documents that attest to the contrary, some of which are:

1. If the Holy Prophet of Islam had derived the Qur'an from the Bible and from the teachings of the prophets before him, the conceptions and contents of the Qur'an would have had to perfectly resemble those in the Old and New Testaments, whereas the purport of the Qur'an is quite different from that of the Old and New Testaments.

2. The magnificent and extremely beautiful wording and style of the Qur'an have brought the greatest literary men of the ages to their knees, proving that the Holy Prophet of Islam has been in direct contact with the Creator of the world. The Holy Prophet could have derived such a style from no other book.

3. No credible authentic source has ever mentioned such false accusations. Rather, these bigoted rumours are made by the Christian clergy and by the western orientalists who have selfish, hostile motives.

4. If the Qur'an had been brought into existence through study of the Old and New Testaments, those intending to fight against the Qur'an through tampering with some of its verses could have more easily made reference to the Old and New Testaments and would have achieved their purpose with a great deal less trouble.

5. All agree that the Prophet was unlettered.[74] Is it logical to believe that an uneducated, unlettered person, brought up in an ignorant, backward society that was devoid of any knowledge, learning or scholarly books could offer such an amazing book, full of startling facts and extremely advanced learning? Such bigoted persons have to be asked, 'How was the Holy Prophet of Islam able to study the Old and New Testaments? How is it possible for an unlettered man who has not been taught by any teacher nor gone to any school, to make predictions of the future and relate events of the past?'

WHAT IS REVELATION?

What is certain is that there have been relations between prophets and the Creator of the universe, that they have received the facts from the original source of creation, and that these relations have had to do with their purified selves and fortified spirits.

It is obvious that if these relations with the divine source were taken away from the prophets, they would have no such supreme position. All the honour and value of the prophets lie in their having relations with the divine source. So there has been no ambiguity in their sayings, and they were all quite sure of what they said and knew very well the Source, Support, and Cause of their words and teachings, unlike those who claim a 'discovery' that might be made as a result of undergoing some ascetic practices. Such people often have no realization of what they have discovered. In fact, their claims are often mingled with fantasy and mere imagination and are sometimes untrue.

The superiority of prophets to such people is so obvious as to need no explanation. Divine prophets have seen and said nothing but the truth, and not even one single unclear, ambiguous point has ever been found in their speeches and teachings. Thus, divine revelation has resulted from a relation between God and His prophets. This relation has sometimes been made through the medium of Gabriel and sometimes directly, without any medium.

IS REVELATION A KIND OF HYSTERIA?

Some western writers who are no doubt prejudiced have been dubious about the descent of revelation upon our Holy Prophet[75] and have considered it a sort of disease called hysteria.

Fortunately, this false accusation is so vain and baseless that it calls for no arguments to prove its falsehood. It is well-known that hysteria has certain moods and indispositions, none of which has been observed in the Holy Prophet of Islam. As John Davenport has said, 'This remark that Muhammad has suffered the attacks of epilepsy is one of the false, awkward sayings of the Greeks by which they meant to stain the prestige of the propagator of a new religion, and turn the world of Christianity against his moral behaviour and qualities.'[76] Even in the deepest moments of revelation, none of the piercing cries of severe agitation common in hysteria have been observed in the Holy Prophet of Islam.

Another reason is that when the person suffering from hysteria recovers from such indispositions, and comes to an ordinary state, that person does not remember anything from what he has seen or heard in his state of hysteria, while the contrary was the case with the Holy Prophet of Islam. He did not speak to anybody during the time revelations came upon him and after each revelation was over, he started talking to the people about the meaning of the revelation and announced everything he had heard or seen. Moreover, the expressions of a hysteric are usually related to the delusions brought about by his suffering and exhausted nerves.

For example, some hysteric people imagine terrible faces that threaten them with death, and their cries are all about such things. And so far nobody has observed a hysteric say something that turns out to be law, knowledge or guidance, like the Islamic rules and teachings that, after 14 centuries, nobody has been able logically to find a single fault with.

REVELATION AND TODAY'S SCIENCE

Unlike what some people might imagine, the advent and advance of scientific discoveries not only have not reduced or damaged the importance or high position of the orthodox religion of Islam, but they have confirmed and supported them.

The inventions of radar, radio, and teletypes have proved the fact that revelation is by no means inconsistent with the laws of nature or incompatible with the secrets of creation. The same God who has provided so many facilities, abilities, and mysterious ways of communication is able to set up special relations and communications with His prophets, though these two sorts of communications are not comparable.

In addition, the advance of the sciences of extra-sensory perception, hypnotism, telepathy and the like have made it clear that the facts of our world are not limited to the framework of our material senses.

Thus both history and science bear testimony to the fact that the Holy Prophet of Islam has been selected by God for the divine mission of leading mankind into the path of virtue and salvation and saving it from the deadly pit of corruption and deviation and that all those excellent ideas and advanced programs were inspired through divine revelation.

The world of Islam is proud of its great leader, the Prophet, whose divine religion not only brought life and prosperity to the world of his own time, but today, after the passing of 14 centuries, is truly the best guide of civilized societies. Each day more and more educated people come to realize the magnificence and value of his profound precepts and teachings.

Chapter 8

The Prophet's Method of Propagating Islam

When the Holy Prophet began descending Mount Hira to go home, he found that he was in a different mood; in a strange mood; in fact in another world; in a divine atmosphere. He was not a prophet before going to the mountain, but now he was related to the Source of Creation, had communicated with the Divine Origin, with the Divine Authority. He was now witnessing what Bahira, the Christian monk, and others had predicted about him, and he well knew that a momentous task had been laid upon his shoulders. He was deeply absorbed by the task. If he had any worries, it was not because he was unsure of his prophethood. He had heard the tidings from such learned people as Bahira, and he had witnessed Gabriel bringing the good news, 'You are God's Messenger'.[77] These were enough to assure him of his divine mission and prophethood.

In addition, God has always, through clear proofs and

compelling confirmations assured any prophet He has selected for guiding mankind of his prophethood, so he would endeavour to rectify, purify, and educate human beings with the strongest determination.

Therefore, it becomes clear that it is most baseless and wrong to say that Muhammad did not know that he had become a prophet until Khadija talked to him and assured him of his prophecy.[78]

KHADIJA WAITING FOR THE PROPHET

What happened on the day of the beginning of the Prophet's prophetic mission caused him to return home later than usual. Khadija, who had never observed her affectionate husband to be late, was worried. Suddenly she saw him enter the house but with quite a new expression and in a new mood. He was now excited and moved. Khadija asked him, 'Why are you so late today?'

He explained the whole event to her. Khadija had long been expecting such a blessed day, for she had heard her servant, Masara, quote from the Christian monk they had met on their journey to Damascus that he, Muhammad, is the Prophet of God to the people.[79]

The Jewish and Christian priests had formerly given her the good tidings that Muhammad was to be a prophet and that he had a supreme status. So she got up and after making the necessary inquiries, contacted Warqa ibn Nawfal, who was a learned Christian person, and told him about the event. Warqa said, 'I swear by God that the same great angel Gabriel who descended to Moses, peace be upon him, has descended unto him, and no doubt he is the prophet of these people, of this *Ummah*'.[80]

Then, to help Khadija realize the extreme significance of the matter, Warqa told her about the signs of the descent of the Angel of Revelation.[81] Khadija then returned home and after brief consideration, accepted the prophecy of Muhammad (peace and the mercy of God be upon him and his descendants), thus attaining the honour of taking the lead in adopting the supreme faith of Islam among all the women of the world.

'ALI, THE FIRST MALE WHO CAME TO BELIEVE IN THE PROPHET'S FAITH

At a time when a severe famine had broken out in Arabia, Abu Talib's financial condition was difficult; indeed unbearable. To reduce his uncle's financial problems, the Prophet took his son, 'Ali, to his own house and took care of him and raised him like an affectionate father.[82] He had great talent and peerless intelligence. He obeyed the Prophet most sincerely. He soon became quite aware of the Prophet's truthfulness, and, so when he was but ten years old, he accepted the Prophet's faith with perfect awareness, thus becoming the first male to adopt Islam and to believe in the divine faith of the Prophet.[83]

THE PRESENTATION OF RITUAL PRAYERS AS A RELIGIOUS DUTY

After monotheism, worshipping the One God, the first duty that became incumbent upon the Holy Prophet and his followers was the ritual prayer, which in fact demonstrates the significance of ritual prayer as the basis of man's relation to God and as a way of giving thanks for God's endless blessings. So the great leaders of Islam, especially the Holy Prophet of Islam, have laid great emphasis on ritual prayer, saying, 'Ritual prayer is the pillar of faith'[84] and 'Anybody who disregards the ritual prayer will not enjoy our intercession with God on the Day of Judgment'.[85]

Almighty God described the nature of ritual prayers and the way to perform them through Gabriel to the Prophet, who taught it to 'Ali and Khadija and also ordered congregational ritual prayers.[86]

THREE YEARS OF PROPAGATION IN PRACTICE

For three whole years after the actualization of the prophetic mission of the Prophet, he propagated his faith in secret because the corrupt environment of Arabia, which had been polluted with idolatry and paganism for centuries, was by no means ready for the open propagation of Islam, which is perfect monotheism and opposed to any kind of polytheism.

In the beginning, the Prophet was faced with extremely difficult problems and obstacles that seemed to prevent him from achieving his divine goal — the propagation of Islam. Thus the Holy Prophet of Islam praised the One God before the eyes of the idolaters who worshipped numerous gods and whose worshipping assumed the form of whistling and clapping. He performed the ritual prayers, which included spiritual discourse and praise of Almighty God, Who has no partner nor any peer. The Prophet, accompanied by 'Ali and Khadija, went to the crowded places like the Masjid ul-Haram and Mana and performed the congregational ritual prayers before the eyes of the enemies of Islam and thus, through his practice, fought polytheistic faiths.[87]

'Atif, a merchant of that time, has said, 'I had gone to 'Abbas, the son of Abdul Muttalib, on business, when suddenly I observed that a man entered the Masjid ul-Haram, looked up at the sky and the sun and stood praying in front of the Ka'aba. A little later, a woman and a boy came in and accompanied him in his prayer. I asked 'Abbas about that religion of which I had not yet heard! 'Abbas said, "This man is Muhammad (peace and the mercy of God be upon him and his descendants), the son of Abdullah. He believes that his God is the Creator of heaven and earth and that God has assigned him to guide people. For the time being his faith has no believers other than these three people. This woman you see is Khadija, the daughter of Khuwalid, and this boy is 'Ali, the son of Abu Talib, who have accepted his faith"'.[88]

In this way the Holy Prophet of Islam went on with his divine task until gradually the number of Muslims increased and, contrary to the ill-wishes of the opponents of Islam, this faith prevailed. When the atmosphere became suitable for the open propagation of Islam, the Prophet was divinely ordered to act accordingly.

THE INVITATION TO HIS RELATIVES AND THE FIRST MIRACLE

The propagation through practice of Islam by the Holy Prophet and the increase in the number of his followers paved the way for the open invitation of the people to Islam. God commanded the Holy Prophet of Islam to invite his close relatives. *'And warn your nearest relatives'* (26:214).

In this way, backbiters could not say, 'Why do you not call your own relatives to worship the One God and warn them of God's severe punishment?' Moreover, the support of the relatives of the Prophet would help the promotion of Islam. So the Holy Prophet told 'Ali to prepare a meal and invite their relatives, who numbered about 40. After preparing the meal, 'Ali invited them. All the relatives of the Holy Prophet accepted the invitation and ate the meal prepared by the blessed hands of 'Ali. Although the food was not sufficient for even one person, all 40 people were full after eating that blessed food and, strangely enough, the food had not diminished at all. This amazed all of them but the obstinate Abu Lahab, who said without thinking, 'This is magic and charms'. The foolish man disregarded the fact that magic and charms cannot feed people!

On that day the Prophet said nothing about the matter. Perhaps his silence was due to the fact that he wanted them to realize the difference between a 'miracle' and 'magic' because if magic were the cause the guests would feel hungry after leaving the house of the Holy Prophet.

Since this gathering did not give any favourable result, the Holy Prophet invited them for the next day. Again the same reception was repeated and all were filled. Yet the food was not reduced even after the meal was over.

Then the Prophet said, 'O sons of Abdul Muttalib. God has

assigned me to warn you of the painful torments of the wrongdoers and give you the good news of His reward to the pious believers. Become Muslims and follow me to achieve salvation. I swear by Almighty God that among all Arabs I do not know anyone who has brought his people anything better than what I have brought you. I have brought you prosperity and salvation both in this world and in the hereafter. The Gracious God has commanded me to call you all to worship Him. Now which one of you is willing to help me with the task? Anybody who announces his readiness to help me will be my brother, my successor, and the executor of my will'.

Nobody answered but 'Ali, who was the youngest. He stood up and said, 'O Prophet of God. I am your assistant. I am your supporter'.

The Prophet asked him to sit down. He repeated the same saying three times but no one except 'Ali replied to him. Then the Prophet pointed to 'Ali and said, 'He is my brother, my successor and the executor of my will among you. Listen to him and obey him'.[89]

It was on this very day that a number of people came to believe in the faith of the Holy Prophet of Islam,[90] but ignorance and bigotry hindered some of his relatives from believing in his message. However, this gathering was effective in gaining support for the Holy Prophet.

In addition to the fact of the extraordinary event — 40 people being fed with a small amount of food — there is another remarkable point in this event — the remarks the Holy Prophet made about his cousin 'Ali on that day. They clearly prove the fact that 'Ali was the Prophet's righteous successor and Caliph, and thus we must regard 'Ali as the successor of the Holy Prophet of Islam.

Thus the way was paved for the public invitation of the people to Islam and open propagation of this divine faith. The Prophet demonstrated indefatigable perseverance in fulfilling this divine duty and did not stop his invaluable teachings, outreach and struggles for a single hour. It was then that the magnificent banner of Islam was hoisted and truth began to be promoted.

Chapter 9

The Public Mission of the Prophet of Islam

Three years had passed from the time when the Holy Prophet of Islam was divinely assigned to be a prophet, during which time he did his best to secretly guide those who were capable of being guided onto the path of piety and virtue. Whenever he observed a person who had gone astray, being drowned in the pit of idol worship and moral decay, he tried hard to save him. He entered the scene through the gate of affection and benevolence and with his logical, eloquent speeches urged the people to adopt the monotheistic faith of Islam.[91]

But since his faith had to prevail all over the world and be communicated to all human beings, he attempted to make his mission public and open and to declare his aims and plans to all.

THE PROPHET'S SPEECH ON MOUNT SAFA
To promulgate the holy religion of Islam to all Arab tribes and all over the world, God commanded the Holy Prophet to openly

declare his prophetic mission and explain to the masses the truth of his faith.

So he made his way to Mount Safa, stood on a high place, and exclaimed, '*Ya sabaha-hu*'.[92] His voice resounded on the mountain and attracted the attention of the people. Large crowds from various tribes hurried toward him to hear what he was going to say. The Holy Prophet turned to them and said, 'O people! Will you believe me if I tell you that your enemies intend to ambush you at dawn or at night?'

They all answered, 'We have not heard a lie from you throughout your life'.

The Holy Prophet said, 'O people of the Quraysh! I warn you to fear God's punishment. Save yourself from the fire.[93] My position is the same as that of the sentry who sees the enemy from afar and warns his people of the danger of their enemies. Does such a person ever lie to his people?'[94]

Abu Lahab, who feared lest the Prophet's words should impress the people, broke the silence and addressing him said, 'Give our oath to you? Have you gathered us here to tell us such words?'

Abu Lahab interrupted the Prophet so rudely and did not let him continue his speech. In return for so much insolence, denial of the truth, and cooperation with the idol worshippers and polytheists, God revealed the verse that severely reproves Abu Lahab.[95]

'In the Name of God, the Merciful, the Compassionate. Perdition overtake both hands of Abu Lahab and he will perish. His wealth and what he earns will not avail him. He shall soon burn in fire that flames and his wife, the bearer of fuel, upon her neck a halter of strongly twisted rope' (111).

THE EFFECT OF THE SPEECH OF THE HOLY PROPHET

The Prophet's logical, eloquent speeches greatly impressed many of the people who heard his words. In most gatherings and public places, people talked about the new faith more than anything else. To those who had suffered from the extortion of the cruel oppressors and were tired of the injustices and inhuman conditions prevailing in Makkah, the celestial words of the Holy Prophet opened a door to the world of hope and prosperity and gave new life to their half-dead bodies. But the selfish malevolent Quraysh chiefs refused to submit to Islam, and, since the Holy Prophet mentioned their deviations and faults at every opportunity, they decided to hinder this spiritual and intellectual revolution by any means possible.

Obviously, the idol worshippers and the oppressive Quraysh chiefs well realized that if idolatry were abolished and all the people worshipped the One God and adopted the gainful religion of Islam, no room would be left for their extortion and oppressive rule.

Therefore, they held a council and started talks on the day's issue, trying to find ways to extinguish the Prophet's revolution.

They reached the conclusion from their talks and exchange of views that they should all go to the house of Abu Talib — a Quraysh chief who was like a father to the Prophet — and ask him to prevent the Prophet from further activities toward propagating his faith by any means he found expedient. For this purpose, they went to Abu Talib, who calmed them down.

THE QURAYSH COMPLAIN TO ABU TALIB

Again the chiefs of the Quraysh went to Abu Talib's house. Their speaker said to him, 'You possess a high status among us and the Quraysh tribe. You are our chief, our master, and our lord. We all have great respect for your honour and high position. We have already asked you to hinder your nephew. We have told you to stop him from offending the faith of our forefathers, denouncing our idols, thoughts and beliefs. But you have not paid any attention to our demands and have not attempted to stop him. We swear by God that we will not tolerate disrespect toward our gods and denunciation of the faith and beliefs of our fathers. You must prevent him from doing these things or we will fight both he and you who support him until either you or we are killed'.

Abu Talib tried to solve the problem peacefully, and after they had left the house, he talked to the Prophet about the matter. Addressing Abu Talib, the Holy Prophet of Islam remarked, 'I swear by Almighty God that even if they put the sun in my right hand and the moon in my left, and in return, demand of me to quit the propagation of Islam and pursuance of my divine aim, I will never do what they want me to. I am determined to carry on my duty toward God to the last moment of my life, even if it means losing my life. I am strongly determined to attain my goal'.

He left his uncle's house sadly. Abu Talib called him and said, 'I swear by God that I will not quit supporting you and will not let them hurt you'.[96]

Once again, the Quraysh attempted to achieve their objectives through Abu Talib. This time they took 'Ammarat ibn Walid to him and said, 'This youth is strong and handsome. We will give him to you to adopt as your own son and in return you must stop supporting your nephew'.

This severely annoyed Abu Talib who gave this answer to their ridiculous request, 'What an unjust proposal! You ask me to take care of your son and give my own son to you to kill him! I swear by God that such a thing will never take place'.[97]

THE QURAYSH TRY TO BRIBE THE HOLY PROPHET

The infidel Quraysh imagined that the Prophet had material or sensual ambitions and that through such ambitions they would be able to induce him to stop his propagation of Islam. With such an intention, they went to him and said, 'If you demand money and wealth, we will make you the wealthiest man among all Arabs. If you are interested in lordship and position, we will make you our absolute chief. If you like sovereignty, we will make you our own sovereign. If you are not able to get over the indisposition you yourself call revelation, we will have the best physican treat you — provided that you quit the propagation of your faith, not create dissension among the people any longer, and not denounce our gods, our thoughts, and the beliefs of our ancestors'.

In answer to those ignorant people, the Holy Prophet said, 'I am neither interested in wealth, nor in lordship nor sovereignty. The One God has assigned me as a Prophet and granted me a Book. I am a Messenger of God and my mission is to warn you of God's severe punishment and give you the tidings of God's reward for the faithful. I have performed my duty. If you follow my instructions, you will achieve prosperity and salvation, and if you refuse to believe in my faith, I will be persistent and resistant until God passes a judgment between me and you'.[98]

Finally, the Quraysh chiefs decided that it would be to their advantage if the Prophet would agree to stop denouncing their gods and idols and, in return, they, too, would stop disturbing him. So again they went to Abu Talib and asked him to talk to the Prophet about their request. The Holy Prophet of Islam answered, 'Shall I not ask them to utter a phrase that is best for them and that brings them prosperity, honour and eternal salvation?'

Abu Jahl said, 'We are ready to utter ten phrases, let alone one single phrase'.

Then they asked the Holy Prophet of Islam what that phrase was. He said, 'There is no god but God'.

This divine strategy severely upset and disappointed the Quraysh chiefs. The obstinate Abu Jahl said, 'Ask for something other than this statement'.

The Holy Prophet of Islam answered with the utmost decisiveness and the strongest determination, 'I will demand nothing other than this, even if you put the sun in my hand'.[99]

Realizing that neither blandishments nor threats would work with him and that they could by no means prevent him from pursuing his goal, the infidel Quraysh chiefs decided to treat him most severely.

Chapter 10

The Obstacles on the Way and the Tortures Inflicted by the Quraysh

From the very day the Holy Prophet of Islam started his public propagation of Islam, the Quraysh chiefs resorted to any means to silence him.

As usual, they first began with attempts to lure him and tried hard to get him interested in wealth, status, and other material benefits that they promised to give him if he submitted to their ungodly will, and, after realizing that this method was of no use in their dealing with him, they attempted to threaten and then to torment and torture him.

Thus a new stage — an exceedingly troublesome phase — started in the blessed life of the Holy Prophet of Islam. The enemies of Islam, who had well understood that the triumph and rule of Islam would surely put an end to their law of the sword, tyrannies, and exploitation of the deprived people, launched their combat against the Holy Prophet of Islam most brutally and ruthlessly, discarding all moral and humane principles — if they had any — and taking up the arms of rancour and cruelty so that they could hamper the spread of Islam and guard the interests of the Quraysh chiefs and men of power.

Of course it cannot be denied that one of the reasons for the opposition of the people of that age to the perfect faith of the Holy Prophet of Islam was their intellectual immaturity. But from the very day the Quraysh tribe heard that the Holy Prophet of Islam called the idols and wooden and stone statues they worshipped valueless and useless, they exhibited the utmost enmity and opposition toward Islam. The Prophet asked the people, 'What do you want with these lifeless objects?.' They were even more enraged when the Prophet denounced the wooden and stone idols of the Quraysh left to them by their ancestors, which they regarded among their ancient glories.

On the other hand, the divine teachings of the Holy Prophet of Islam were inconsistent with the interests of the oppressive class of the chiefs of the Quraysh who wanted to continue exploiting the poor people and possessing innumerable slaves, as well as with the interests and inhumane desires of the usurers who wished to amass wealth at the expense of the deprived class of their society.

It goes without saying that in an environment where no divine law is obeyed and no human right is respected, the strong will forcibly violate the honour, property, and chastity of the defenceless people, and so the new faith — Islam — which severely opposed and fought this wrong social system, enraged those whose interests and selfish considerations were endangered.

Such notorious people as Abu Jahl, Abu Sufyan, Abu Lahab, Aswad ibn Abd Yaghwan, 'As ibn Wa'il, 'Utbah and Shaybah, Walid ibn Maghirah, and 'Aqibah ibn Abi Ma'ayyat were among the leaders of the opponents of Islam.

Cruel, false accusations, physical torment, foul language, economic and financial pressure and boycotts were among the inhumane methods used by the Quraysh chiefs against the Prophet and his faithful companions.

Here some examples of the offences and torments which the enemies of Islam inflicted upon the Holy Prophet are mentioned:

1. One day a number of Quraysh gave the uterus of a sheep to their servants to throw at the blessed face and head of the Prophet. They obeyed their brutal master, thus making the Prophet rather sad.[100]

2. Tariq Maharibi has narrated, 'I saw the Holy Prophet saying in a loud voice to the people, "O people! Say there is no god but God so you would find salvation".

'He urged the people to submit to Islam and become monotheists while Abu Lahab followed him step by step and threw stones at him injuring him so that his feet were covered with blood, but the Holy Prophet continued to guide the people and show them the path of eternal salvation and prosperity. Abu Lahab cried out, "People! This man is a liar. Do not listen to him".'[101]

3. In addition, the Holy Prophet of Islam, as well as his loyal friends and those who had newly adopted Islam, were most severely tortured and tormented by the infidels.

One day, the Holy Prophet of Islam observed 'Ammar Yasir and his family being tortured by the enemies of Islam. Addressing 'Ammar and his faithful family, he said, 'I give you, 'Ammar's family, the good tidings that Paradise will be your eternal abode'.[102]

Ibn Athir has written, 'Ammar and his parents suffered severe tortures from the idol worshippers. The idol worshippers forced them out of their house in the hot burning weather and tortured them under the burning rays of the sun, inflicting the most unbearable tortures upon them so that they would leave the faith.'

Sumayyah, 'Ammar's mother, was the first woman martyr of Islam, killed by a blow from Abu Jahl's weapon. Yasir, 'Ammar's father, too, died under the torture of the infidels. 'Ammar himself was most cruelly tortured by the enemies of Islam but resorted to dissimulation and thus saved his own life.[103]

4. Bilal, an Ethiopian slave, was among the Prophet's most faithful followers, and, because of his faith in Islam, his ruthless master brutally tortured him. At midday when it is scorching hot, his master would make Bilal lie down on the burning hot desert pebbles and sand and put a large and heavy stone on his chest to force him to stop obeying the Holy Prophet of Islam and to worship their idols instead of worshipping the One God.

Bilal resisted all his threats and tortures most bravely and admirably and responded just by repeating the word 'Ahad' (One), meaning 'God is One and Peerless and I will never become an idol worshipper'.[104]

Unfortunately, there is no room in such a relatively small book to narrate in detail all the sad stories of the Muslims of early Islam. Thus we content ourselves with observing that the enemies of Islam resorted to any means at their disposal in their fight against Islam and the Muslims, some of which were:

Economic struggle: The Quraysh had started a fierce economic struggle against the Prophet and his followers. One of the inhumane weapons they used against the Muslims was economic pressure and boycott of any sort of transactions with the Muslims.

Psychological warfare: Prohibiting of marriage with Muslims, cutting off all relations with them from the Quraysh, and accusing the Holy Prophet of Islam of witchcraft, telling lies, and the like were psychological tactics meant to break down the resistance and perserverance of the first Muslims.

Physical torment and torture: Another anti-human method of fighting the new movement and its adherents used by the Quraysh was physical torture of the Muslims, which resulted in the martyrdom of a number of faithful Muslims at the beginning of Islam.

In spite of all the brutal methods that the infidel Quraysh utilized in their struggles against Islam, the Holy Prophet and the Muslims, Islam advanced and the Prophet continued to urge the people to go the right way. Islam and the Muslims continued their efforts and struggles.

To maintain their faith in Islam, the Muslims underwent extremely severe torture, sufferings, and hardships and showed admirable resistance in following this honorable path.

A careful and just survey of the conditions of the Muslims at the beginning of Islam reveals the significant fact that, unlike the picture the enemies of Islam have always tried to present, Islam, this holiest of faith, has not been promoted at the point of the bayonet or by the sword, but for 13 years, the Holy Prophet of Islam and the faithful Muslims tolerated the tortures, torments, and swords of the infidels and the idol worshippers to promote this divine religion revealed by God for their salvation.

Chapter 11

The Migration of the Prophet: the Source of Historical Transformation

GOING INTO EXILE TO ACHIEVE THE DIVINE GOAL

The Holy Prophet of Islam was well aware of the fact that people who were plunged in prejudice, superstition, and ignorance would not abandon their beliefs and ways easily and that it would take extensive struggle, severe hardships, and sincere self-sacrifice to save them from the pit of corruption and guide them onto the path of virtue and monotheism. He could easily read in the faces of the people of Makkah, the opposition to Islam and their bigoted determination to fight the Muslims.

The divine foresight of the Holy Prophet of Islam had given him a dark image of the future. With such an insight and divine knowledge, he held high the banner of prophecy and adopted patience and tolerance. The Prophet struggled with the enemies of Islam in Makkah for 13 years and resisted all their torments and obstructions, but the opponents of Islam did not give up their devilish beliefs and manner and utilized all their power to destroy Islam.[105] Under such circumstances, the universal mission of the Holy Prophet of Islam necessitated his migration to a calm, suitable place and to find a new arena for his work and mission.

YATHRIB — READY TO SUBMIT TO ISLAM
At the time of the pilgrimage to the Ka'aba, some of the men of importance of the Khazraj tribe came to Makkah and met with the Holy Prophet in the Masjid al-Haram. He explained the divine faith of Islam to them and encouraged them to believe in this religion, which is the faith of peace and fraternity. The Khazraj chiefs, who were tired of their deep-rooted disputes and conflicts with the Aws tribe, felt that Islam was exactly what they needed, and so they most willingly submitted to Islam.

When the Khazrajis, who had become Muslim, were about to return to Yathrib, they asked the Holy Prophet of Islam for a missionary, and he assigned Mas'ab ibn 'Umir to accompany them. Thus, the people of Yathrib were informed of the rising sun of Islam and hurried to gain information about the new faith.

The most effective factor in making the people ready and eager to adopt Islam was listening to the luminous verses of the Holy Qur'an. Mas'ab reported the conversion to Islam of the chiefs and leaders of both the Khazraj and Aws tribes to the Holy Prophet. Later on, a large number of the people of Yathrib who had come to Makkah to take part in the Hajj pilgrimage held a secret meeting with the Prophet at midnight and swore allegiance to support him just as they supported and protected their own families.[106]

THE PLOT TO MURDER
THE HOLY PROPHET OF ISLAM
Dawn had hardly broken when the infidel Quraysh were informed of the allegiance of the Yathribi Muslims. They

hurriedly attempted to frustrate it and hinder the advance of Islam. For this purpose, they held a council in the place where the Quraysh gathered to pass judgment and to consult each other. After a great deal of talk and consultation, it was resolved that they select one man from each tribe to rush into the house of the Prophet at night and murder him so that the basis of the propagation of Islam would be destroyed.[107]

But Almighty God made the Holy Prophet aware of the intrigue of his enemies and commanded him to leave Makkah by night.[108] The Prophet, upon receiving this revelation, decided to leave his homeland and migrate to Yathrib.

'ALI'S SELF-SACRIFICE
When the Holy Prophet of Islam was divinely commanded to migrate to Yathrib, he called 'Ali, disclosed his secret to him, gave him the people's trusts to be returned to their owners and then said, 'I have to migrate, but you must lie in my bed'. 'Ali sincerely obeyed the Holy Prophet and lay in his bed, thus devotedly exposing himself to the dangers that threatened the Holy Prophet of Islam.[109]

'Ali's self-sacrifice was so sincere and significant that God praised it in the Holy Qur'an.[110]

THE HOLY PROPHET OF ISLAM GOES TO THE THAWR CAVE
At midnight the enemies of Islam surrounded the house of the Holy Prophet to carry out their satanic plot. But since God was the supporter and protector of the Prophet, He saved him from harm at the hands of the murderous infidels.

While reading verses from Sura Yasin, the Holy Prophet of Islam came out of his house and through a by-way, went to the Thawr cave, which was situated outside Makkah. Abu Bakr was informed of the matter and accompanied the Holy Prophet.[111]

The infidels rushed towards the Prophet's bed with drawn swords in their hands, but to their surprise, they found 'Ali in his place. Upset and enraged, they asked, 'Where has Muhammad gone?' 'Ali answered, 'Had you assigned me to watch him? Well, you intended to expel him and he has left the city'.[112]

Realizing that all their plots were frustrated, the idol worshipping Quraysh took serious measures but all in vain.

ON THE WAY TO YATHRIB

After staying in the Thawr cave for three days, the Holy Prophet of Islam proceeded towards Yathrib.[113] One of the Makkans, Saraqa ibn Malik, attempted to pursue him, but his horse's hoof sank into the ground three times and threw him down, so he repented and returned to Makkah.[114]

On the 12th of Rabi al-Awwal, the Holy Prophet of Islam reached a place called Quba,[115] where he stayed for a few days.[116] Abu Bakr insistently asked the Prophet to begin travelling towards Yathrib, but the Holy Prophet refused to go without 'Ali. He said to Abu Bakr, 'Ali has endangered his own life to save mine. He is my cousin, my brother, and the dearest among the family to me. I will not leave here until he joins me'.[117]

After fulfilling the mission assigned to him, 'Ali joined the Holy Prophet in Quba, but his legs were so bruised that he could hardly walk. The Holy Prophet embraced him most affectionately, blessed his hurt legs with the saliva from his own mouth which healed 'Ali's swollen legs. Thus together they started towards Yathrib.[118]

YATHRIB EAGERLY AWAITING THE HOLY PROPHET

Yathrib had taken on an extraordinary air and intense excitement and eagerness had overtaken the whole city. In every alley and neighbourhood people impatiently awaited the Holy Prophet of Islam.

He entered Yathrib on Friday.[119] People were overjoyed and could not stop looking at the resplendent countenance of the Prophet.

The Holy Prophet of Islam settled in Yathrib and there laid the foundations of Islam and a magnificent culture based on justice and faith.

After the blessful entrance of the Holy Prophet of Islam into Yathrib, its name was changed into Medinat ul-Nabi, meaning 'the City of the Prophet'.[120] That year, the year the Holy Prophet of Islam migrated from Makkah to Yathrib, was recognized as the origin of history, due to this significant historical event, the triumph of righteousness and justice. The illuminating sun of Islam gave new life to the people. They discarded all the old superstitious beliefs and thoughts and all the wrong deeds and manners of the past, replacing them with the perfect life-giving culture of Islam.

A LESSON FROM THE HIJRA

14 centuries have now passed since the momentous historical event of the Hijra — the migration of the Holy Prophet from Makkah to Medina. A careful study of history reveals the sincere and indefatigable efforts of the Muslims in the cause of the migration and laying the foundation of Islam.

After migration to Yathrib, the migrant Muslims had obviously rid themselves of the torment and torture of the infidel Quraysh and found a peaceful, agreeable environment. Nevertheless, they showed no tendency towards self-indulgence and pleasure-seeking. Rather they ceaselessly endeavoured to establish an Islamic civilization and to spread the divine faith of Islam.

It was these very sacrificial efforts and hard work of the Muslims that rescued them from slavery and so many miseries and brought them honour, prosperity, and glory.

It is indeed necessary for the Muslims all over the world to be constantly reminded of the devotion and incessant efforts of the Muslims in the early days of Islam, who relied on their faith in

God and, through obeying the instructions of the Holy Prophet, managed to make a holy revolution and attained great achievements. It is of vital significance to Muslims in all places and at all times to take a lesson from the lives and sacrificial endeavours of those truly devoted Muslims. Each year, on the occasion of the anniversary of the migration, sincere reflection on the lives of these godly men and women will effectively serve this purpose.

It is also incumbent upon us to teach posterity the fact that the Muslims of the beginning of Islam owed their glory and greatness to their faith and their sincere efforts and that we must try to adopt their manners if we want to regain the honour and greatness that devoted Muslims really deserve.

Chapter 12

Laying the Foundation for an Islamic Fraternity in Medina

The existence of sympathy, sincerity, and harmony among the people of a society makes that society a living one — one that is fit for human life and evolution, in which all can find salvation and progress and can enjoy each other's sympathy and sincerity.

In the process of establishing such an ideal human society, Islam does not pay the least bit of attention to such considerations as race, language, skin colour, and geographical location. Rather, this holy religion regards all Muslims as equal.[121] It looks only at the people's faith in God, which is the root of all unity.

'Islamic brotherhood' is the phrase best revealing this all-embracing unity. This meaningful, clear expression in the Holy Qur'an describes this Islamic precept: *'Truly the faithful are brothers'* (49:10).

THE PROPHET'S INITIATIVE IN CREATING ISLAMIC BROTHERHOOD

After having settled in Medina and after building a mosque that was indeed the military and constitutional base of the Muslims, the Holy Prophet of Islam took an excellent initiative. He laid the foundation of Islamic brotherhood, so that great unity and sincerity would be engendered in Muslim society and so that the emigrant Muslims would know that, though they had lost a number of their friends and relatives and had been forced to leave their homes, in return, they had gained brothers who were much more loyal and sympathetic from every point of view.

Therefore, besides the general fraternity and brotherhood that exists among all Muslims, the Prophet concluded contracts of brotherhood among his followers. He announced each two Muslims to be brothers. He himself selected 'Ali as his own brother and said, "Ali is my brother'.[122]

In the Holy Qur'an, Islamic brotherhood has been elevated and held in reverence: *'And hold fast to the covenant of God, all together, and remember the favour of God upon you when you were enemies, then He united your hearts so by His favour you became brethren, and you were on the brink of a pit of fire, then He saved you from it; thus does God make clear to you His communications that you may follow the right way'* (3:3).

ISLAMIC BROTHERHOOD: BYWORD OF UNITY AND FRATERNITY

Islamic brotherhood is not a honorific expression but a reality mingled with the spirit of faith whose fruits emerge one after the other.

Our Holy Leader Imam Sadiq has explained some of the fruits of Islamic brotherhood in the following way: 'A believer is the brother and guide of another believer. He does not betray or oppress him, nor does he ever cheat his brother. A believer never breaks his promise'.[123]

One of the requirements of Islamic brotherhood is that whatever a Muslim desires for himself, he should desire for his brother in Islam, and he should help his Muslim brothers by any means possible, whether by his wealth or by his speech or by any other means. It is far from Islamic brotherhood if you have enough food, water, and clothing while another Muslim is hungry, thirsty and naked.

Imam Sadiq, peace be upon him, has said, 'If you have a servant and your brother in Islam does not have any, you must send your servant to help your brother prepare food, clean clothes, and perform any other needed work'.[124]

Islamic fraternity has overshadowed all relationships, even family relationships. The Qur'an openly says, '*You shall not find a people who believe in God and the latter day befriending those who act in opposition to God and His Apostle, even though they were their own fathers or their sons or their brothers or their kinsfolk*' (58:22).

It was the principle of Islamic brotherhood that made the Ethiopian Bilal and the Persian Salman brothers and two of the best companions of the Holy Prophet of Islam. In the light of Islamic brotherhood, many deep-rooted enmities were reconciled and divided groups were united. This unity requires that all Muslims share each other's sorrows and joys like members of a large family. Muslims should be sincere and affectionate toward each other, and their watchword should be unity and brotherhood.

Islamic brotherhood firmly holds all Muslims responsible toward each other and establishes an all-embracing responsibility so that Muslims cannot be heedless of each other's troubles and problems but every Muslim must, within his own abilities, endeavour to solve the problems of Muslims and to create possibilities for the advancement and promotion of Islam.

This responsibility is divided into two parts:

Economic Cooperation: This responsibility is related to meeting people's economic needs, such as hygiene, education, shelter, employment, and the like, and part of the precepts of the Holy Qur'an and the instructions of religious leaders deal with this as well as with fundamental precepts and programs such as *zakat* (the poor-due prescribed by Islam), almsgiving, charity, and the like.

Scientific and Educational Cooperation: This part includes propagation, guidance, and teaching. That is to say, all Muslims are duty-bound to communicate to others whatever they have learned and not to neglect each other's guidance. Also, there are two basic principles among the practical precepts of Islam that urge Muslims to call upon each other to perform their religious duties and to refrain from committing sins. These precepts, which are indeed most beneficial to Muslims, are rated among the most significant requirements of Islamic brotherhood. But unfortunately, Muslims seem to have forgotten this great precept due either to imaginary fears or to selfish interests, and perhaps due to both.

As we clearly observe, in most Muslim societies, prohibition from committing sins and mutual encouragement to obey religious instructions have long been neglected. This deplorable situation has resulted in the ruin of the ethical spirit of Islamic brotherhood, and following this ruin, other superiorities and advantages of this living society are lost.

ISLAMIC BROTHERHOOD IN THE PRESENT AGE
In our age, Muslims need real unity more than ever. God has endowed Islamic countries with invaluable resources which others intensely covet. Thus, they try every means possible to divide Muslims and distract them from their critical situation. It goes without saying that dispersion, lack of unity, and negligence are extemely effective causes of ruin and slavery, and obviously the world-devouring enemies of Muslims are quite aware of this fact.

Therefore, we Muslims must be alert and vigilant in order to overcome those who clearly intend to exploit us, devour our natural resources, and bring us humiliation and misery.

The solution to our problems concerning our brutal enemies lies in Islamic brotherhood of which the foundation has been laid by the blessed hands of the Holy Prophet of Islam, and in following Islamic precepts.

No matter how powerful the Muslims are, still they greatly need unity. So the lesson of unity and Islamic brotherhood should be effectively taught to primary school students, and later on, as youngsters grow older and are promoted to higher grades, practical training programs treating Islamic brotherhood and other precepts of Islam must be added to their education, to strengthen their Islamic spirit. Moreover, it is one of the greatest duties of Muslim parents to bring up children who are real Muslims and sympathetic to other Muslims.

It is crystal clear that if the Muslims had observed the principles of Islamic brotherhood and had been united and sympathetic, they would never have suffered so much tyranny, humiliation, and exploitation from the non-Muslims. But it is a pity that the Muslims' negligence has given the covetous exploiters an opportunity to enslave, humiliate, degrade, and plunder millions of Muslims in Africa, Asia, and all over the world, Muslims who really deserve lordship and superiority if they follow Islamic precepts.

Chapter 13

Jihad: Religious and Spiritual Struggle in the Way of God

More than 1,000 million Muslims in different parts of the world unitedly celebrated the beginning of the 15th century of the actualization of the prophetic mission of the Holy Prophet of Islam.

This celebration was held to glorify the great day when the Prophet hoisted the flag of peace and brotherhood and laid the foundations of universal peace and peaceful co-existence; just as Almighty God has said to the Prophet, '...*And We have not sent you but as a blessing to the worlds*' (21:107).

Islam has best resolved the racial and class differences that are the causes of most wars, conflicts, and disastrous events, whereas the so-called civilized world of today is deeply involved in bloody wars and ruinous conflicts and each day the world's murderous statesmen and supercriminals find a new pretext under which to fan the flames of war.

Islam's care for peace and justice is so great that in the Qur'an, the followers of the Book, the Jews and the Christians, have been explicitly urged to adopt unity and harmony in the moving expression, *'Say: O followers of the Book! Come to an equitable proposition between us and you that we shall not serve any but God and (that) we shall not associate aught with Him...'* (3:74).

When the Muslims migrated to Medina and the flag of victory was hoisted over their heads, numerous peace proposals were offered to the Prophet by his opponents and he welcomed them. An undeniable testimony to this fact was his peace agreements with several Jewish tribes that were concluded in the first year of the Hijra.[125]

THE PURPOSE OF JIHAD

Islam is a dynamic, comprehensive school that aims at the rectification of the social and economic systems of the world in a special manner.

Unlike the beliefs of the ancient Romans, the Jews, and the Nazis, Islam is not restricted to a certain community or a certain race, but is for all human beings and aims at human prosperity and salvation. This divine faith requires all Muslims, guided by the holy precepts and instructions of Islam, to endeavour to rescue the oppressed masses, to establish peace and justice, and to acquaint the unaware people of the whole world with Islam and Islamic rules and regulations.

The combatants of Islam do not intend to gain control of a land or overthrow an oppressive rule to replace it with a similar rule through jihad. Rather, jihad is a pure humanitarian struggle fulfilled in God's way and for human evolution and the rescue of the oppressed people. This struggle culminates in the elimination of all sedition and in the establishment of peace and prosperity.

This great undertaking and the dynamic precepts of Islam put an end to the negligence and degradation of large groups of people, just as they end the oppressive rule and tyrannical lordship of those who live in luxury at the expense of the poor and the defenseless.

Human nature urges that the corrupt members of society be destroyed like weeds so the way may be paved for human salvation and prosperity and so the oppressed may be released from the tyranny of the oppressor. Humanitarian, justice-loving, and noble people adhere to this holy struggle and embark upon it.

GOD'S WORDS
'And were it not for God's repelling some men with others, the earth would certainly be in a state of disorder, but God is gracious to the creatures' (2:251).

In the theory of Islamic law, war is not an end in itself, but it is regarded as the final means of hindering tyranny and aggression and paving the way towards salvation for mankind.

Once the spokesman for the Arab Muslims said to Rustam Farrokhzad, the Iranian military commander, 'God has assigned us to lead the people who worship other people into worship of the unique, peerless, One God, to urge them to leave a degrading life for a noble one and to rescue them from the torments of false religions through Islamic justice. We will let go of the land of any people who accept our invitation to Islam and will go back to our own land."[126]

DID ISLAM PREVAIL BY
THE FORCE OF THE SWORD?
As a matter of fact, through jihad, the Muslims have mainly meant to establish connections with the people who are under the oppressive rule of tyrants, so the oppressed masses would become acquainted with Islamic rules and precepts and so they would comprehend the glory and genuineness of independence and salvation. The Muslims are well aware of the fact that the oppressed masses will most willingly accept Islam as the best divine faith if Islam is correctly explained to them.

In fighting the infidels, the Muslims did not force people to become Muslims but gave them the choice to retain their own faith provided they submitted to the conditions of peace. In return, the Islamic government would protect them.

In the peace agreement of Hudaybiyah, the Holy Prophet of Islam undertook that no Muslim would shelter any of the infidel Makkans[127] even if they became Muslims before or at the time of seeking refuge with the Muslims in Medina and would return them to Makkah, and he stood by his promise.[128] If the Holy Prophet had wished, he could have taken the same promise from his enemies that if a person left Islam and sought refuge with the infidels of Makkah, he would be returned to Medina.

When Makkah was conquered by the Prophet and his followers, he gave the Quraysh freedom of choice. He did not force anybody to adopt Islam. He wanted them to become Muslims as a result of their true understanding of Islam and of their own free will, not by force. He ordered the Muslims not to kill anybody in Makkah except for a few who were constantly causing trouble for the Muslims.[129]

When the infidels asked him for refuge, he would give them refuge and the opportunity to study Islam and then to submit to it freely. For instance, Safwan ibn Umayyah fled to Jeddah when Makkah was conquered by the Muslims. When some people asked the Holy Prophet for refuge on his behalf, he sent his turban for him as a sign of refuge to give him immunity on returning to Makkah. Safwan returned from Jeddah and asked the Prophet to give him a respite of two months. He agreed to his request and gave him a respite of four months. And Safwan accompanied the Holy Prophet of Islam to Hunayn and Ta'if and finally discarded infidelity and submitted to Islam of his own free will.[130]

CONCLUSION

We conclude that in Islam, the sword is resorted to only in dealing with those who have realized the truth and yet fight it and thus try to hinder others from achieving salvation, and that force is applied to banish tyranny, to release the oppressed, and to create favourable conditions for human progress and evolution.

The sincere and loyal faith of the Muslims at the beginning of Islam and their resistance to all torture and hardship are themselves the best testimonies to the fact that Islam was not promoted by force. History bears witness to this reality: that the Muslims at the beginning of Islam were so devoted to their faith that they persevered in it through their struggles no matter what torture and torment the infidels inflicted upon them. Many of them even left their homeland and migrated to other places.

The Ethiopian Bilal was among those who took the lead in accepting Islam. Abu Jahl made him lie on the burning hot pebbles, placed a heavy stone on him, the torture of which is, needless to say, beyond endurance. When the faithful Bilal was being tormented, Abu Jahl shouted at him, 'Disbelieve in Muhammad's God. Discard Islam.' But Bilal just repeated, 'The One. The One',[131] meaning God is the One, and 'I worship the One God'. In fact Bilal, as well as many other faithful Muslims at the beginning of Islam, suffered a great deal from the enemies of Islam who had aimed most obstinately at the destruction of Islam.

All of them tolerated all the pains and torture and did not leave their faith even for a single moment. We see therefore very clearly how the accusation that Islam prevailed by force and by the law of the sword is false and far from the truth.

Having found no weak point in Islam, the opponents of this divine religion obviously resorted to such accusations to stain Islam, unaware of the fact that Islam prevails because it is the most supreme divine faith, perfectly compatible with human nature. It gives shelter to the oppressed, deprived masses and presents solutions to all problems facing human beings, whether they be in the material, spiritual, emotional, educational, or political realms.

A Frenchman has written, 'Islam easily prevailed, and this should be rated as one of the special characteristics of Islam. Islam persists forever wherever Muslims step'.[132]

Another Christian writer has written: 'The commercial and cultural contacts beyond the borders of Islam have by far been more effective in the expansion and promotion of the Islamic world than have been military conquests'.[133]

Chapter 14

The Motives of the Wars of the Prophet

Unlike the self-centered rulers and kings all over the world who embark on wars for expansionist purposes, for the exploitation of human powers, and for the plunder of other people's wealth and natural resources, the Prophet of Islam refused to resort to the sword and fighting unless it was necessary and unavoidable. Instead, he advanced carrying the torch of the Holy Book and the divine laws and would get involved in war only to remove the stumbling blocks — the thorns in the way of salvation — to hinder oppression and tyranny, and to hoist the flag of justice and truth.

The battles of the Prophet of Islam against the infidels were, needless to say, meant to remove those brutal selfish pagans from the scene who for the sake of their own satanic passions and desires inflicted all kinds of oppression against God's pure creatures and prevented the promulgation of Islamic precepts and beliefs. He only fought to bring about conditions of justice and equity under which human beings could materialize the ideology of world peace and mutual understanding.

Can such a war be considered illegitimate and unjust? It goes without saying that such struggles are necessary and that no Prophet could avoid combating those who intend to bring ruin on human societies and cause corruption and social decay. No doubt any wise, humanitarian person accepts such combat and admires it because there is no other way to achieve the sacred ends of the Prophets.

Jesus Christ, peace be upon him, had a short prophetic life and lived under conditions that did not permit war, so he did not attempt any wars. Otherwise, he too would have destroyed the weeds and troublemakers of human society.

Christian propaganda purposely misinterprets the holy wars of the Prophet of Islam and ascribes large numbers of casualties to them to weaken the morale of Islamic nations, to hinder the ever-increasing expansion and prevalence of Islam, and to make the murder of millions of innocent people by the masters of churches and in the crusades appear trivial and negligible to the people of the world.

Here we will first point out the motives of the Prophet of Islam in the wars he undertook, and then we will briefly cite the casualties of all the wars at the time of the Prophet, so the truth may be made clear. In this way, readers can realize the philosophy of Islamic wars for themselves and can also see that the casualties of these holy wars were trivial in comparison with those of other wars.

THE WAR OF BADR

For 13 years after the advent of the prophetic mission of the Prophet of Islam, he and his followers were tormented and tortured by the infidel Quraysh in Makkah. Finally, the Prophet of Islam left Makkah and migrated to Medina. Yet the infidel Makkans did not stop tormenting the Muslims who had remained in Makkah and also did not let them leave Makkah and migrate somewhere else.[134]

At the same time, the Makkan enemies of Islam had decided to put Medina under a severe economic siege. They had forbidden all caravans from carrying provisions and foodstuffs to Medina. This siege lasted such a long time that the people of Medina were faced with many troubles and hardships and had to go as far as the coasts of the Red Sea to buy foodstuff.[135]

Abu Jahl, too, wrote an extremely harsh and rude letter to the Prophet of Islam and in that letter warned him to expect the attack of the Quraysh.[136]

It was on this occasion that God said, *'Those who have been expelled from their homes without a just cause except that they say, "Our Lord is God." Had there not been God's repelling some people by others, certainly there would have been pulled down cloisters and churches and synagogues and mosques in which God's name is much remembered; and surely God will help him who helps His cause; most surely God is strong, mighty'* (22:39-40).

In the second year of the Hijra, the Holy Prophet of Islam arose to guard Islam, to defend the basic rights of the Muslims, and to frustrate the satanic conspiracies of the Quraysh. In the war of Badr, they confronted the Quraysh troops. Though the number of Muslim combatants was one-third that of the infidel forces, the Muslims defeated the infidels by their power of faith and by God's help.[137]

THE WAR OF UHUD

Since a considerable number of the infidel troops had been killed in the Badr war, the next year, the third year after the Hijra, the Quraysh prepared for war to take revenge for their defeat in the Badr war. They proceeded to Medina. They faced the army of Islam in a place called Uhud. Since a number of the Muslims in the war did not fully obey the instructions of the Holy Prophet, the Muslims did not become victorious in the Uhud war.[138]

THE AHZAB (TRENCH) WAR

In the fifth year of the Hijra, a Jewish tribe called Bani Nazir went to Makkah and incited the Quraysh against Islam and the Muslims. The Quraysh took advantage of the opportunity, gathered a huge army from different anti-Islamic groups, and started toward Medina.

To guard Medina, the headquarters of Islam, the Muslims dug moats all around the city and lined up in front of the enemy army, whose number amounted to 10,000. 'Ali, peace be upon him, overcame and defeated their commander, and finally the war ended to the advantage and victory of the Muslims.[139]

THE BANI QURAYZAH WAR

The Bani Qurayzah[140] had concluded a peace agreement with the Holy Prophet of Islam, but they violated that agreement in the war of Ahzab and rendered help to the Quraysh.[141] Since the Prophet had recognized them as a 'dangerous' people, the Muslims had no choice but to kill them.

After the war of Ahzab, the Prophet ordered his army to proceed against the Bani Qurayzah. For 25 days, the Bani Qurayzah were besieged by the Muslim army, and they finally surrendered.

The Aws tribe asked the Holy Prophet of Islam to forgive them and spare them the punishment of death. He asked them, 'Are you ready to select Sa'ad Ma'az, who is one of the men of status among you, as the arbiter and accept his arbitration?' They all agreed, hoping that Sa'ad would take their side. But Sa'ad Ma'az's verdict was to kill their fighters, to take their possessions as booty, and to take their women captive.

The Holy Prophet said, 'The arbitration of Sa'ad Ma'az is the same arbitration God has passed upon such people'. Then all their fighters were killed.[142]

THE BANI MUSTALAQ WAR

The Bani Mustalaq were a group of the Khaza'ah tribe who

took measures against the Muslims. The Holy Prophet of Islam came to know their plots and proceeded against them with his combatants to repel their brutal assault, fought them in a place called Maris'a, and defeated them. This war occurred in 6 A.H.[143]

THE KHAYBAR WAR
Large numbers of Jews lived in the Khaybar forts and had military and economic relations with the infidels. Since the security of the Muslims was constantly threatened by those anti-Islamic Jews, in 7 A.H. the Muslims started towards Khaybar, which was the headquarters of the enemy, surrounded the fort, and, after a triumphant war, made the Jews submit to the Islamic government.[144]

THE MUTAH WAR
In 8 A.H., the Holy Prophet of Islam sent Harith ibn Umar with a letter to the king of Basra, but his messenger was killed in a place called Mutah.[145] At the command of the Prophet, the army of Islam marched towards the enemy, and in Mutah they confronted the army of Marqal, the king of Rome. His army comprised 100,000 Roman and non-Roman fighters. A war broke out between the two armies in which Zayd ibn Harith, Ja'far ibn Abi Talib, and Abdullah ibn Rawahah, the three famous commanders of the army of Islam, were martyred, and the Muslims could not overcome the infidels, so they returned to Medina.[146]

THE CONQUEST OF MAKKAH
In the Hudaybiyah peace agreement, the Quraysh had promised the Holy Prophet of Islam not to transgress against or oppress the Muslims and their confederates, but they violated the agreement and helped the Bani Bakr tribe to destroy the Khaza'ah tribe, which was one of the confederates of the Muslims. To hamper their aggression, the Prophet approached Makkah in secrecy, entered it through an elaborate device, and conquered the city. Then he made a pilgrimage to God's House

— the Ka'aba — and delivered a historic speech in which he declared, 'You should beware that you have been bad neighbours for God's Prophet. You refuted us, tormented us, expelled us from our homeland, and yet did not content yourselves with so much torture and troublemaking; you even did not let us have peace in Medina and attempted to fight us. But in spite of all this, I set you all free and let you go unpunished'.[147]

This great tolerance and forgiveness brought about the submission of the people of Makkah to Islam. In this triumphant battle, the Prophet ordered the Muslims not to fight for any reason other than defense and against the violations of the infidels. However, he passed a death sentence upon eight men and four women, and conflict arose between the army of Khalid and a number of infidels who had fought under the leadership of Akramah ibn Abu Jahl in which a number were killed.[148]

HUNAYN AND TA'IF
The Havazin tribe had gathered an army against Islam. The Holy Prophet was informed of their satanic intentions and mobilized 12,000 Muslim soldiers to confront them. The two opposing armies fought each other in the valley of Hunayn, and finally the Islamic army defeated the army of the infidels and subdued them.[149]

After this victorious war, the Prophet attempted to fight the Saghif tribe, who had conspired with the Havazin against Islam, but after having besieged it for a while, he dispensed with its conquest and returned to Makkah.[150]

Some other less severe wars also took place between the army of the Holy Prophet of Islam and the infidels, and also several journeys for the propagation of Islam were made during these blessed times.

Now the data on casualties, from both the Muslim army and the infidel's army, of all the wars that took place between the Muslims and the infidels are presented, having been gathered from credible documents.

The Names of the Wars	Tarikh Khumays	Sirat ibn Hisham	Tarikh Yaqubi	Tabaqat	Bahar al-Anwar	Tarikh Tabari
Badr	84	84	86	84	84	84
Uhud	93	92	90	109	109	70
Ahzab	9	9	14	11	9	9
Bani Qurayzah	800	850	750	700	900	850
Bani Mustalaq	12	—	—	10	10	—
Khaybar	32	23	—	98	—	3
Mutah	21	13	—	13	—	3
Makkah	39	20	—	33	—	21
Hunayn and Ta'if	96	101	—	87	112	85
Other wars	250	122	—	119	333	210

Notes:
1. This data has been presented, observing, in the case of differences, the maximum numbers, and we have left blank any place for which we have not found any data.

2. *Tarikh al-Khumays* is one of our sources of acquiring data and is a collection of tens of books on commentary, *ahadith* (traditions of the Prophet of Islam), and history.

It goes without saying that, in comparison with the casualties in the crusades of the Christians, those of the Islamic wars against the infidels are trivial, and also there is no doubt, therefore, that none of the wars of the Holy Prophet of Islam were launched out of motives of expansion, revenge, or aggression. Rather, they were aimed at the replusion of the aggressors, defense of the honour of the Muslims, and independence and the exaltation and prevalence of right, truth, and justice.

A Frenchman relates, 'While Islam has made it incumbent upon Muslims to make jihad, it has ordered Muslims to treat the followers of other faiths with tolerance, justice, and remission and has given them freedom of religion'.[151]

Chapter 15

The Universal Mission of the Prophet of Islam: A Faith for both East and West

Islam emerged like a limpid fountain and increased in depth and expanse as time went by. It finally became a great river passing through various human societies, irrigating fields in which seeds of humanity were to be planted, satisfying the thirst of human beings for salvation and justice. It is going on and will surely continue to do so as long as there are human beings on earth because human nature is thirsty for this heavenly faith and would perish if it were denied it. Islam is truly the only power that is able to wipe out all wrong manners, all corruption, and all corrosive attitudes in all places and at all times and to lead human beings onto the path God has determined for them.

Obviously, Islam does not please those who oppress, the colonialists, the arrogant, and their like. So they have always tried hard to hinder it, but in spite of so many wicked policies and plots of the world-exploiters and despite the serious attempts of the enemies of Islam to misrepresent this holy faith, Islam has prevailed.

Islam contains the secret of victory as well as of prosperity. The fact that Islam is a divine faith, not a man-made one, is testimony to the rightful claim that all the laws, rules, instructions, and precepts necessary for human happiness and salvation are to be sought in it.

Is it not the case that God has created human beings as well as all other beings? Is it not the case that the Creator knows all about His creatures? Is it not true that the same gracious God who has created so many wonderful natural resources to meet human material needs has also endowed human beings with divine resources to satisfy their spiritual wants?

Thus being presented by God, it is totally compatible with human nature and consistent with all human wants and needs: material, spiritual, and emotional. Most important of all, it provides all the necessary means for human evolution towards salvation so that when man leaves this world for the eternal one, he will be deserving of Paradise there and not hell, just as God wants man to be. It goes without saying that all laws and precepts in the holy faith of Islam have been made on the basis of human nature, which is the same in all human societies and at all times. So those who say, 'East is east and west is west' and 'An eastern Prophet cannot be a good leader for western people', are absolutely wrong. For human beings, whether of the east or the west, have their nature, their natural characteristics, and their wants in common. There is no difference between people in this respect, no matter how different their race, colour, traditions, geographical conditions, and the like may be. And just as eastern people need an innate faith — a faith compatible with their nature and capable of satisfying their various human needs — western people are in need of such a divine faith, exactly to the same extent. A simple comparison can serve to clarify the matter. Human beings all over the world and at all times need food, water, and oxygen to survive, and there is no human being found without a need of them for his survival. Just so, all of them need spiritual nourishment for their souls, their emotional health, their spiritual survival, and, most significant of all, their finding salvation.

There are, of course, many proofs to this righteous claim that Islam ensures human happiness and salvation in all parts of the world, and at all times. Those who oppose this divine faith and try to misrepresent it are in fact the greatest enemies of human beings.

MAKKAH: THE STARTING PLACE FOR THE PROPHET'S PROPAGATION OF ISLAM

It is crystal clear that when the Holy Prophet of Islam illuminated the dark atmosphere of Makkah with the call of monotheism, he did not mean to lead just the people of the Hijaz or the Arabs, but his divine mission was to communicate God's message to the whole world and to start this momentous task from Arabia.

One proof of this true belief is that at the beginning of his mission, he said to his own relatives, 'Truly, I am God's Messenger to you, in particular, and to all people, in general...'.[152]

There are also some verses in the Qur'an that confirm this claim. Consider the following three verses: *'Say, O people, "Surely I am God's Messenger to you all"'* (7:158). *'And We have not sent you but as a mercy to the worlds'* (21:107). *'And this Qur'an has been revealed to me that with it I may warn you and whomsoever it reaches'* (6:19).

Such verses reveal the fact that the divine mission of the Prophet was not revised to become universal after his migration to Medina and the prevalence of Islam. From the very beginning, his holy mission was meant for all people, for all parts of the world, and for all times.

In answer to the question asked of Imam Sadiq, 'Why is the

Qur'an always new and fascinating no matter how many times it is read or taught?', he said, 'God has not sent the Qur'an for a special time or for a particular group. The Qur'an is for all and forever, so till doomsday it will be new and enchanting at all times and to all groups of people'.[153]

ANOTHER TESTIMONY TO ISLAM'S UNIVERSALITY

In 6 A.H., the Holy Prophet of Islam dispatched several representatives to rulers and kings of different parts of the world, each with a letter in which he invited them to become Muslims and submit to God's faith. All these letters had the same purport, that is, the invitation to monotheism and Islamic fraternity.

Since the Holy Prophet's mission was divine, in obedience to God's command, consistent with human nature, and meant to lead people to God's path, it highly impressed such just, truth-seeking people as Najashi, Muquqs, and others, so they submitted to Islam.[154]

Research made on the collection of the Prophet's letters indicates that he sent 62 letters to kings, chiefs of tribes and clans, and heads of convents. The texts of 29 of these letters are available.[155]

Now we will take a glance at parts of the letters of the Holy Prophet of Islam.

A LETTER TO KHUSROW, THE KING OF IRAN

In the Name of God
the Merciful, the Compassionate

From Muhammad, God's Messenger, to Khusrow, the King of Persia. Greetings to the followers of the right path, to those obedient to God and His Prophet, to those who bear witness to God's Oneness, who worship the One God, and who bear witness to the prophecy of God's servant, Muhammad.

Truly I call upon you to obey God's command and convert to

Islam. I am God's Messenger to all the people so that living hearts will be awakened and illuminated and so that infidels will have no excuses. Submit to Islam so you will be safe and immune, and if you disobey me and turn down my invitation, you will be blamed for the sins of the magi.[156]

A LETTER TO HARQAL, THE KING OF ROME

*In the Name of God
the Merciful, the Compassionate*

...I call upon you to submit to Islam. If you become a Muslim, you will share the Muslims' gains and their losses, and if you do not want to become a Muslim yourself, then let your people freely convert to Islam or pay the poll tax, paid in lieu of conversion to Islam, and do not restrict them in choosing their faith.[157]

The letters of the Holy Prophet of Islam were not exclusively written to kings. Rather, he sent letters to various nations and to the followers of other faiths so all would be informed of the rising of the sun of Islam.

A LETTER TO THE RULER OF YAMAMAH

*In the Name of God
the Merciful, the Compassionate*

This is a letter from God's Messenger, Muhammad to Hawzah. Greetings to the one who follows the path of salvation and the instructions of the divine guides.

You, the ruler of Yamamah, note that my faith will advance to the farthest place where man can go, so submit to Islam to be immune.[158]

A LETTER TO THE JEWS

*In the Name of God
the Merciful, the Compassionate*

This is a letter from Muhammad, God's Messenger, Musa ibn 'Imran's brother and co-missionary. God has assigned to Muhammad the same mission He had assigned to Moses. I swear to you by God and by the sacred commands descended upon Moses on Mount Sinai that: Have you found in your Holy Book predictions of my prophetic mission to the Jewish community as well as to all other peoples? If you have found this, then fear God and convert to Islam, and if you have not found such a divine prediction, then you will be excused.[159]

A LETTER TO BISHOP NAJRAN

In the Name of God
the Merciful, the Compassionate

This is a letter from God's prophet Muhammad to Bishop Najran: Truly I call on you to worship the real adored God instead of worshipping God's creatures.[160]

OUR DUTY IS TO CONVEY THE MESSAGE OF ISLAM

The speedy advance and promulgation of Islam were due to the sincere, indefatigable endeavours of our Holy Prophet more than anything else.

In the propagation of Islam, the Holy Prophet utilized two powerful, effective forces: one, proficient speakers who had realized the truth and righteousness of Islam and who deeply loved and admired the Holy Prophet of Islam, and, two, the amazingly impressive letters, which revealed the vivifying precepts of Islam and which, in reality, were crystal clear reflections of Islam. He sent his messengers to different parts of the world although there were many hardships in their way and the needed means and facilities were scarce or unavailable.

Now the holy soul of our Prophet is worried about Muslim societies, and no doubt he watches them to see how they attempt to promote Islam, to communicate the precepts of Islam to people all over the world, and also to see if they make use of modern technologies and media to propagate the holy teachings of Islam.

So it is incumbent upon us to mobilize all our forces and powers to promote the cause of Islam and to spare no effort or self-sacrifice in the propagation of this holy faith, so our eastern and western brothers and sisters in Islam may be led to this vivifying fountain of truth. It will be a great achievement for us to have the honour of such an invaluable service to Islam and to humanity in general. Just as our Holy Prophet said to 'Ali, 'I swear by God that if God leads a person towards salvation through you, it will be more valuable and beneficial to you than the value of all the beings in the whole world upon which the sun casts its rays'.[161]

Chapter 16

Muhammad, the Last Prophet

All Muslims of the world, no matter what their sects are, hold in common that the Holy Prophet of Islam was the last prophet, and in fact, Muslims believe in divine prophecy having ended with him, just as they believe in the Unity of God.

Islam is always fresh, wonderful, and comprehensive, and the more extensive is one's insight, the more one comprehends the comprehensiveness of Islam. As a matter of fact, there is no end to Islam's wonders and miracles.

Now let us survey the truth of this belief. First we will explain the most effective reasons for a faith being eternal, and then we will consider Islam.

The most important factor causing a faith to persist and enjoy perpetuity is its being consistent with and based on human nature. A religion of which the instructions are in accordance with natural and innate human characteristics will continue to prevail forever, will never suffer annihilation as a result of the passing of time, nor will such a faith become out of date and useless.

Instructions and precepts that are not restricted to a certain place or period of time are compatible with any kind of progress and will stay as valid and powerful as they have always been no matter how many changes take place in the material aspects of human life and how much advance is made in technology and natural sciences.

On the contrary, instructions and rules that are limited to a particular period or a special group fail to fulfill all aspects of human needs at all times and under all circumstances. For example, if a rule is made that commands people are only allowed to use natural vehicles such as horses and camels for traveling and transportation, such a rule will obviously be discarded and outdated because new necessities make people utilize new means and equipment. One of the reasons why past faiths are not durable is that they have been meant for a certain group or a special period of time.

Comprehensiveness: An eternal faith must be all-embracing, comprehensive, and able to meet all human needs and wants. It is an already experienced fact that man's thirsty, stormy soul does not find peace and satisfaction with a series of empty ceremonies but is in great need of comprehensive precepts and rules that are capable of guiding him all through his life, of providing solutions to his various problems both in personal and social life, and of satisfying his spiritual demands and wants.

Giving guidance in deadlocks: There are certain occasions in human life when either due to the conflict of general rules or due to an unexpected emergency, man finds himself in a deadlock and starts wondering what to do and how to proceed.

Thus an eternal faith must, in addition to overall rules and instructions, provide man with other sets of rules and guidelines that explain the solutions to exceptional problems and emergency situations that general rules are incapable of handling.

And it is such a comprehensive faith that is in accord with all times and all conditions of life and can benefit all. In fact, it is only a perfect faith that serves the supreme purpose of leading human beings onto God's path. The foregoing factors are the most significant causes of the duration and perpetuity of a faith all of which are in Islam. Now let us find some explanations for these factors.

ISLAM: THE IMMORTAL FAITH

It is a reality that, in the legislative system of Islam, human nature, which is the same at all times and in all places, has been taken into consideration and positive answers have been given to natural human wants and needs. A careful study of Islamic precepts and programs reveals the fact that they have been so designed as to regulate all human instincts. For example, for the proper satisfaction of human sexual instincts, various simple plans and rules have been offered that properly satisfy and regulate this natural instinct at the same time that they prevent unrestrained sexual relations, so human societies may be immune from the corruption and decline that sexual freedom causes.

The fundamental rules and laws in Islam are meant not just for a particular time or a particular place needing modification and change as conditions change, they are compatible with all environments and all times and are capable of providing human beings with all the guidelines they need to live happily and prosperously and to find eternal salvation as well.

In the Islamic programs and teachings concerning jihad, for instance, no emphasis is placed upon weaponry and tactics of the time of the Prophet, such as fighting with swords. Rather, Islam has given this general command concerning jihad: Strengthen your fighting abilities, mobilize your forces, and acquire good arms and ammunition so you will be able to defend your vital rights against your enemies and overcome them. This is a general all-embracing rule that is in accordance with all conditions of life and all sorts of progress made in technology. And thus this comprehensive rule can invariably give guidance on the questions concerning war in Islam, and the same is the case with other Islamic rules and instructions.

To the deadlocks and emergencies that occur in human life, either individual or social, the faith of Islam has offered laws such as 'the law of emergency', 'the law of not guilty', 'the law of no loss',[162] and the like, which present suitable solutions to all problems, however complicated they might be. Moreover, the Imams, the successors of the Holy Prophet of Islam, and religious leaders whom Muslims follow can offer decisive solutions to social deadlocks and problems.

The programs and rules designed by Islam are far more extensive and elaborate than those presented by other schools of thought. In Islam, all legal, economic, military, moral, and other issues and points have been presented and surveyed in the most elaborate and perfect manner. The Islamic theologians have so far compiled thousands of books on the fore-going subject for which the sources are the Holy Qur'an, the sayings of the Holy Prophet of Islam, and the teachings of the offspring of Prophet.

Thus, taking into consideration these facts and proven realities, any knowledgeable person will admit that Islam is a perfect faith, capable of fulfilling human needs and of presenting solutions to all problems, and so there is no need for any other faith or any new school of thought.

THE END OF PROPHECY WITH THE PROPHET

The comprehensiveness of the rules and precepts of Islam and the end of prophecy with the Holy Prophet of Islam have been clearly expressed in the Qur'an: *'And the word of your Lord has been accomplished truly and justly; there is none who can change His words, and He is the Hearing, the Knowing'* (6:115).

'Muhammad is not the father of any of your men, but he is the Messenger of God and the Last of all Prophets, and God is

cognizant of all things' (33:40).

In the Arabic language, wherever the word *'khatam'* is attached to a word, it conveys the meaning of 'the last' and in this verse it refers to 'the last of the prophets'. *Nabi* means any type of divine messenger.[163]

Obviously, the word messenger can be applied to all prophets so by saying that Muhammad is the last of all prophets, God means that he is the last of all messengers and that after him there will come no prophet, nor any messenger from God, nor any person with a new holy book.

'Surely this Qur'an guides to that which is most upright and gives the good news to the believers who do good that they shall have a great reward' (17:9).

Therefore, human beings have no need for any other prophet, any other rules and regulations, or any other school of thought because all they need is to be found in the Qur'an.

There are so many documents and testimonies to the fact that the Prophet was the last of all prophets that in Islam this reality is considered one of the clearest points.

Now your attention is drawn to some narrations:

The Prophet has himself said, 'You must know that there will come no Prophet after me and no faith after my faith of Islam...'.[164]

Imam Baqir (peace be upon him) has said, 'God has ended Holy Books with your Book, the Qur'an, and prophets with your Prophet...'.[165]

Hazrat 'Ali (peace be upon him) has said, 'God assigned Muhammad, peace and the mercy of God be upon him and his descendants, to be a prophet after all other prophets and has ended revelation with him'.[166]

The Prophet said to Hazrat 'Ali, 'Your relation to me is like that of Aaron to Moses, peace be upon him, with the difference that there will come no prophet after me'.[167]

Imam Riza (peace be upon him) has said, 'The faith of Muhammad (peace and the mercy of God be upon him and his descendants) will not be abolished until the Day of Resurrection, and no prophet will come after him until that day'.[168]

These and many other traditions and narrations are perpetual proclamations of the Prophet as the last of all prophets and Islam as the only comprehensive faith.

The splendour of the purport of this faith as well as its profound precepts and comprehensive rules ensure its perpetuity till the Day of Judgment.

Now that God has endowed us with such a matchless magnificent faith, surely it is our duty to communicate it to all other people so all will benefit from this holy faith.

Chapter 17

Ghadir and the Prophet's Successor

It was in 10 A.H. and the time for Hajj. The Hijazi deserts witnessed large crowds of Muslims who unitedly chanted the same slogans and proceeded towards the same holy end.

That year the sight of the Hajj pilgrimage was much more exciting and moving than ever before. Muslims most hurriedly and eagerly traversed the way and went to Makkah — this holy city.

The celestial melody of *'Labayka'*, 'Yes, I have come', resounded through Makkah. Caravans reached the city one after the other. The *hajjis* unitedly and harmoniously in pilgrim's garb, while shedding tears of joy and love for God, hurried to the sacred threshold of God and circumambulated the Ka'aba — the Holy House built by the champion of monotheism — Abraham, the Friend of God.

Farid Vajdi has calculated the number of *hajjis* to have been 90,000[169] in the year 10 A.H., but there are some who hold that the number was 124,000.[170]

The Holy Prophet of Islam watched that splendid scene with the utmost affection and eagerness. He was pleased to observe that the Masjid al-Haram was overflowing with Muslims who had gathered together in conformity with the holy precept, *'Truly the faithful are brothers'*, and were worshipping God like brothers and angels.

The Holy Prophet was clearly happy with his great achievement — with having fulfilled his divine mission in the best manner possible.

Nevertheless, his resplendent face was sometimes covered with a halo of sorrow and anxiety, and his pure heart filled with sadness and worry.

He was in fact worried about the fate of the Muslims after his leaving this world for heaven. He feared lest after him the society of Muslims should break apart; Muslims should disperse, the spirit of unity and fraternity should vanish among them, and consequently they regress.

Obviously, the Holy Prophet of Islam was well aware of the fact that the *Ummah* of Islam was in great need of honest, knowledgeable leaders, or otherwise the fruits of his years of efforts would all be wasted.

For this reason, whenever he was going to leave Medina either for war or for other purposes, even if his trip was short, he would assign a competent, trustworthy person to supervise their affairs and would never leave the people of Medina without any guardian and supervisor.[171]

Thus, how is it possible to imagine that such a compassionate, sympathetic prophet might have left the momentous affairs of his beloved *Ummah* of Islam to chance and not have designated any reliable administrator for them.

And no doubt he knew very well who deserved the position of the caliphate of the Muslims and for whose mature stature the garb of the caliphate had been sewn.

That celebrated man was the same who, in the presence of the chiefs of the Quraysh and the relatives of the Prophet who had been invited to the House of the Prophet of Islam at the beginning of his prophetic mission, had been acknowledged as the successor of the Holy Prophet of Islam by the Prophet himself.[172]

He was a pious, God-fearing man who did not associate anything with God and did not prostrate before idols even for a single moment.

He was a sacrificial soldier of Islam. His knowledge originated in the knowledge of the Prophet of God and his judgment was the best.[173]

He was well-known. He was 'Ali, son of Abu Talib.

The Hajj ceremonies were over, and the Muslims were preparing to move towards their own towns when suddenly the call of the herald of the Holy Prophet of Islam resounded in the Hijaz desert and made the Muslims stop. His heralds called on the people to gather together again.

The Muslims, of course, did not know why they had been given this command, but the fact was that the Angel of Revelation had descended and conveyed this verse to the Prophet, *'O Prophet! Deliver what has been revealed to you from your Lord; and if you do it not, then you have not delivered His message, and God will protect you from the people; surely God will not guide the unbelieving people'* (5:67).

The issue about which God spoke to His Prophet in such a serious tone was nothing other than the formal announcement of the caliphate of 'Ali, the significant subject that the Prophet hesitated to declare, for he feared lest this announcement should cause dissension and discord among the Muslims and was thus waiting for a favourable occasion to make clear the matter to them.

Upon receiving this revelation, he knew that the time had come for the crucial purpose. So he immediately assembled the Muslims at Ghadir Khum, which was a hot, arid desert, to clarify the vital issue in Islam — the issue of the caliphate.

The people started wondering why that command had been issued, but before long the congregational ritual prayers was announced and after saying the noon ritual prayers, the crowd of Muslims witnessed the celestial, enchanting countenance of the Prophet over a pulpit made of saddles of camels.

A profound silence prevailed. Then the divine, meaningful words of the Prophet broke the silence of the Hijaz desert. After praising Almighty God, he announced the heart-rending news of his oncoming death and then asked the Muslims, 'O people! What kind of a prophet have I been for you?'

All exclaimed unitedly, 'O Prophet of God! You did your best to admonish and rectify us and never neglected to train us and led us onto the path of piety. May God reward you best'.

The Holy Prophet of Islam said, 'After me, God's Book and the sinless leaders are side by side your leader and guide. You should perfectly follow them, so you will not go astray'.

Then he took 'Ali by the hand, lifted him so that all would see him and exclaimed, 'O people! Who is the guardian and supervisor of the faithful?'

The Muslims answered, 'God and His Prophet know best'.

The Holy Prophet of Islam said, 'God is my Master and I am the Master of the faithful'. Then he added without any pause, "Ali is the Master of those whose Master I am. Almighty God be the friend of his friend and be the foe of his foe. Help those who help him and frustrate the hope of those who betray him...'.

The Prophet repeated the sentence, "Ali is the Master of those whose Master I am', three times. At the end of the speech he said, 'Those present should convey this truth to those who are absent'.

The crowd of Muslims had hardly dispersed when this verse was revealed to the Prophet, *'This day have I perfected for you your religion and completed My favour on you and chosen for you Islam as a religion'* (5:3).

After the magnificent ceremonies of designating the successor of the Holy Prophet of Islam were over, the Muslims hurried to congratulate 'Ali for being appointed as the Prophet's successor and Caliph.

Abu Bakr was the first to congratulate 'Ali and 'Umar was the second. They parted with 'Ali while saying the following words, 'Blessed are you, son of Abu Talib, who have become my Master and every believer's Master'.[174]

THE NARRATORS OF GHADIR

As a matter of fact, there are more than 120,000 narrators of Ghadir. According to the command of the Prophet, the Muslims present at Ghadir regarded the incident of Ghadir and the issue of appointing 'Ali as the successor of the Prophet as most significant and narrated it to the others.[175] And it was for this reason that in public gatherings of Muslims, the reminiscence of Ghadir was renewed repeatedly.

About 25 years after the day of Ghadir, when most of the faithful companions and followers of the Holy Prophet of Islam had passed away, and just a few were still alive, 'Ali asked the people to bear witness if they had been present in Ghadir and heard the Ghadir tradition from the blessed mouth of the Prophet. Immediately 30 people stood up and narrated the Ghadir tradition.[176]

In 58 or 59 A.H., a year before the death of Mu'awiyah, Imam Husayn, peace be upon him, assembled the Bani Hashim and Ansar and other *hajjis* at Mana and, during an extremely moving speech, asked them, 'I swear to you by God to speak out if you know that on the day of Ghadir, God's Prophet appointed 'Ali as the Master and Leader of the *Ummah* of Islam and commanded the audience to convey this message to the others'. All said that they knew this fact.[177]

Sunni scholars have mentioned in their reliable books the names of 110 companions of the Prophet who had heard this tradition from the Holy Prophet of Islam and had narrated it to others.[178] Even a number of scholars and Islamic theologians wrote special books on Ghadir.[179]

THE PURPORT OF THE DISCOURSE ON GHADIR

The available documents reveal that the words *mawla* (master) and *vali* (guardian) refer to the successor of the Holy Prophet of Islam and the Guardian of the *Ummah* of Islam, and that no other meaning can be applied to these two words.

Now, take notice of the following points:

We have realized that the Holy Prophet of Islam was hesitant to propound the Ghadir tradition and that he did not declare it until God openly and seriously commanded him to do so.

It is totally wrong to hold that by the Ghadir tradition the Prophet meant to remind the people of the position of 'Ali as a friend of the Holy Prophet of Islam and the Muslims. If that were the case, the Holy Prophet of Islam would never have hesitated to announce it, for obviously such an announcement would cause no discord or dissension among the Muslims.

Thus the Holy Prophet of Islam surely had reference to the issue of the caliphate and the assignment of his own successor, which was clearly likely to elicit the mutiny and mischief of ambitious opportunists.

Before uttering the well-known sentence, "Ali is the Master of those whose Master I am', the Prophet asked the audience to admit that he himself was their guardian and leader and that he was to be obeyed by them, and after the people present in Ghadir Khum had admitted this fact, the Holy Prophet of Islam attributed the same position to 'Ali immediately, saying "Ali is the Master and Leader of anybody whose Master and Leader I am'.

With the permission of the Prophet, Hissan ibn Sabit composed a poem about Ghadir Khum and circulated it. In this poem, the position of the Caliphate and Imamate of 'Ali have been openly expressed and specified. No one among that great crowd of Muslims protested that Hissan had misapplied the word *mawla* (master). Rather, Hissan was confirmed and applauded for this poem.

The poem, in effect, said, 'After the Holy Prophet of Islam had the people admit that he was their divine Master and religious leader, he said to 'Ali, "Stand up, 'Ali. I assent to your Leadership and Imamate after myself. Then, "Ali is the Master and Leader of anybody whose Master and Leader I am. You should all be loyal followers and sincere friends of 'Ali'".[180]

After the Ghadir ceremonies were over, the Prophet, together with 'Ali, sat in a tent and ordered all the Muslims, even the women of his own family, to congratulate 'Ali, to swear allegiance to him, and to greet him as the Commander of the Faithful.[181] It is obvious that all these ceremonies and orders testify to nothing other than the designation of 'Ali as the Caliph and Imam of the Muslims by the Holy Prophet of Islam.

Twice the Prophet said to the people, 'Congratulate me, for God specifically appointed me Prophet and my family Imams'.[182]

These testimonies and documents leave no doubt about the Ghadir Khum tradition and the caliphate of 'Ali.

Chapter 18

The Morals and Behaviour of the Holy Prophet

The more science and technology advances, the greater is the need for the observance and practice of the teachings and instructions of divine prophets in human societies. This is because science and technology provide only machines and instruments and by no means prevent their misuse by human beings.

The terrible rise in murder, other felonies, corruption, suicide and so forth clearly points to this very fact. If morality, which is a significant part of the teachings of divine prophets, does not prevail and govern in human societies, surely not only will advanced science and technology fail to ensure human peace and prosperity, but they will add to our problems and miseries. For the exploiters and colonialists utilize advanced technology and sciences for their own satanic purposes. They murder or make homeless millions of human beings as they have always done and trample upon the rights of the weak and the defenseless.

As a matter of fact, the only factor that can halter man's restive soul and control his stormy instincts and passions and thus utilize science and technology for human prosperity and pacific life is true morality, which originates in faith in God.

The moral teachings and precepts of the divine prophets and their moral behaviour are the best means of leading man to his ideal life. It goes without saying that both in personal and in social life the observance of moral principles is required of all. However, for those who must lead societies and guide the people, this requirement is much greater, because, first, the one who is the instructor of society must himself be a model of supreme moral behaviour and excellent human characteristics, so he will be able to wipe moral decay out of people's hearts and minds. Obviously if he himself is lacking in morality, he will fail to lead the people onto the path of humanity and virtue.

Second, the responsibility of leading human societies is so great and crucial that no one can successfully perform it unless he has perfect morals. For this reason, God selected his prophets from among those who possessed exalted spirits, great tolerance, extraordinary patience, and other excellent moral characteristics. It was with this weapon of morality that divine prophets overturned the debased societies that were plunged in corruption and led the ignorant people who had gone astray onto the path of virtue and salvation.

In the holy Qur'an, God has addressed the Prophet Muhammad: *'Thus it is due to mercy from God that you deal with them gently, and had you been rough, hard-hearted, they would certainly have dispersed from around you'* (3:159).

The sublime celestial morals of the Prophet brought about the waves of the revolution of Islam first in Arabian society and afterwards all over the world. In the light of this all-embracing spiritual and intellectual resurrection, dispersion turned into unity, unchastity into chastity and virtue, idleness into hard work and industry, selfishness to altruism, and Arab arrogance to modesty and affection. Men and women were thus trained to become models of good moral behaviour and have altruistic manners forever. The morals of the Prophet were so sublime and praiseworthy that God has regarded them as great. *'And truly you (Muhammad) possess great morals'* (52:4).

THE PROPHET AMONG THE PEOPLE
The Holy Prophet of Islam possessed the magnificent status of prophecy and divine leadership, but his manners in dealing with the people and his way of life were so simple and gentle that when he was among the people and a newcomer wanted to know about him, he had to ask, 'Which one of you is the Prophet'?[183]

He had no love for luxuries or the illusions of this mortal world. He was never enchanted by any worldly things, and he invariably looked upon this world's life as a passing one.[184]

The Holy Prophet of Islam spoke in short, meaningful sentences and was never seen or heard to interrupt anybody's speech.[185]

He never spoke with a morose face, nor did he ever apply rough, awkward words. Unlike tyrants and despotic rulers, the Holy Prophet of Islam never looked at those who were addressing him with half-closed eyes.[186]

The Holy Prophet of Islam did not care to sit down in the seat of honour in gatherings, and on entering any place would sit down in the first empty seat available.[187]

He did not let anybody stand up before him and treated others most respectfully. Of course, the virtuous people were most revered by him.[188]

The Holy Prophet was justly angered when he observed a violation of God's commands and of Islam and was most pleased at the good deeds. Both his pleasure and displeasure were for God. He would never allow anybody to accompany him on foot when he himself was riding. He would pick him up beside himself if he was able, and if not, the Holy Prophet of Islam gave him a time for an appointment in a given place and would ride alone.

On group journeys, the Prophet would work like the others and would never let anybody work instead of him. Once on a journey, his companion asked him to allow him to do the work. In answer to this request, the Holy Prophet of Islam said, 'I do not like to be treated as if I were privileged because God does not like any of His creatures to consider himself privileged or to be treated as if he were privileged over others'. And he got up and collected firewood.[189]

He invariably stood by his words and pledges. He paid affectionate visits to his relatives and friends but would never take their side unduly. The Holy Prophet of Islam would never permit anybody to backbite others and said, 'I want to meet people with a loving heart'.

His modesty was peerless. He was extremely patient, tolerant, and forgiving.[190]

Anas ibn Malik, who was the servant of the Holy Prophet of Islam, has narrated, 'I used to prepare milk for the Prophet to break his fast with. One night he was home late. Thinking that he had been a guest at somebody's house and thus had broken his fast there, I drank the milk. Before long he returned home. I asked his companions if he had broken his fast and they said that he had not.

'When the Holy Prophet of Islam was informed of the matter, he made no remark about it and behaved as if he were not hungry at all and went without supper with a cheerful face. The next day he also fasted.'[191]

The Holy Prophet of Islam immensely loved the ritual prayers, but on occasions when people demanded to talk to him about something, he would say his ritual prayers briefly and instead, pay attention to the demands and needs of the people. He would spare no efforts to fulfill the people's needs.

The Prophet treated everyone with great respect and considered nobility and honour to be owing to faith, piety, and good behaviour. He was not interested in wealth or status, nor did he revere anybody for his riches or position.

His behaviour towards slaves was amazingly affectionate, and he would do his best to remove the troubles and sufferings of the slaves and the poor.[192]

THE PROPHET'S TOLERANCE AND FORGIVENESS

The Holy Prophet of Islam never attempted to retaliate against the insults and disrespect of anybody, and forgave people's mistakes or their misconduct. His reaction to the torment and disregard of the ignorant people was forgiveness and tolerance.[193]

In spite of all the tortures and torments that the Quraysh had inflicted upon the Holy Prophet of Islam, on conquering Makkah, he forgave them and set them free.[194]

In the war of Uhud, a man named Wahshi killed Hamzah, the beloved uncle of the Holy Prophet of Islam. However, he forgave his sin. Also, he forgave the many torments and troubles that Abu Sufyan and his wife, Hind, had caused for him and he did not take revenge.[195] However, for all his tolerance and mercifulness, he did not take pity on those who violated God's threshold and sacred precepts and would punish the violator in accordance with divine rules. In affecting God's orders, he would take no notice of anybody's intercession.

When the Prophet was informed that Fatima Mukhzumiyah had committed theft, he punished her according to the laws of Islam concerning theft and did not regard the intercession of Asamata ibn Zayd in this respect, saying, 'The ruin and downfall of the preceding peoples was due to the fact that they did not enforce the laws of punishment in the case of the aristocrats and the people of status. I swear by the One in

Whose hands is my life that even if Fatima (his daughter) had committed such a sin, I would cut off her hand'.[196]

THE PROPHET'S CLEANLINESS AND ORDERLINESS

The Holy Prophet of Islam was fond of scent[197] and spent more on buying perfumes than on food.[198] His pleasant smell filled the air of any place he passed, so that whosoever passed there knew that the Holy Prophet of Islam had passed that way.[199]

He used to brush his teeth frequently[200] and washed his blessed hands both before and after meals.[201] Whenever the Holy Prophet of Islam was about to leave his house, he would look into a mirror or into water; he always left home with a clean, pleasant appearance.[202]

THE PROPHET WAS A PIOUS AND SINCERE WORSHIPPER OF GOD

The Holy Prophet of Islam had great love for ritual prayers so that during the night he would get up several times, brush his teeth, and then offer the most devoted prayers.[203] He would stand worshipping God and talking sincerely to the Almighty Creator for so long that as a result of so much standing in prayer, his legs were swollen.[204]

The Holy Prophet of Islam took lessons from watching the sky, the moon, the sun, and every other thing in nature, and these phenomena attracted him to their Creator more than to themselves.

He was so devout and pious that not even for a single moment was he enchanted by any luxury or pleasure of this mortal world. In short, the Holy Prophet of Islam was a perfect model of all excellent virtues and sublime human qualities.

In such a small book it is not possible to describe all his praiseworthy manners and morals. In fact, we have just presented a pale reflection of his celestial, resplendent portrait so that all over the world Muslims who regard themselves as the followers of Islam can make his morals and conduct their own model of behaviour and learn divine morality and correct programs for life from him.

As the Holy Qur'an says, *'Certainly you have in the Apostle of God an excellent exemplar for he who hopes in God and the latter day, and remembers God much'* (33:21).

May God's greetings be upon him who was the selected superior and the best of pious human beings. And the greetings of the angels upon the faithful.

We too greet him most cordially and sincerely. May he accept our respectful greetings as well as the greetings of you, our sisters and brothers in Islam. May Almighty God help all of us to follow exactly the blessed footsteps of the Holy Prophet, whose path is sure to lead us into eternal salvation and paradise.

To end this book, we narrate an invaluable tradition of the Holy Prophet of Islam and his honoured family. In the Holy Qur'an there is a verse closely related with the Tradition of the Cloak: *'And stay in your houses and do not display your finery like the displaying of the ignorance of yore; and keep up prayer, and pay the poor-due (zakat) and obey God and His Apostle. God only desires to keep away the uncleanliness from you, O people of the House! and to purify you a thorough purifying'* (33:33).

This verse is famous as the *ayat-i-tathir* and is closely related with the Tradition of the Cloak. The following is the tradition:

One day the Holy Prophet of Islam came to the house of his daughter, Fatima, and told her that he was very tired and asked her to cover him with his cloak. As she was covering the Apostle of God, his face lit up and shone like the full moon. After a while Imam Hasan came to the house and said that he could smell the fragrance of his grandfather. Fatima said that he was resting under the cloak. Hasan greeted the Holy Prophet and asked his permission to come under the cloak. The permission was granted. Similarly, Husayn, 'Ali, and Fatima, after greeting him and receiving permission from the Apostle, went under the cloak. Fatima, peace be upon her, said that when they, the *ahl al-bayt*, gathered under the cloak, Almighty God said, 'Let it be known to you, my angels and those who are in the heavens, that I swear by my honour and might that I have not created the heavens and the earth and what are in them, but only out of love for the five honourable ones who are under the cloak'.

Gabriel asked God who was under the cloak. God informed him that they were the people of the house of the Apostle. Gabriel requested permission from God to be the sixth under the cloak. Gabriel greeted the Prophet and received permission to enter under the cloak. Gabriel said that God has created the universe because of them and out of love for them. And '*God only desires to keep that which is ritually unclean away from you, O people of the House, and to purify you a thorough purifying*'.

'Ali asked the Holy Prophet to explain the significance of their gathering under the cloak. The Prophet said, 'I swear by God that whenever this tradition will be recited among our friends and lovers, God's mercy will descend upon them and the angels will surround them and ask forgiveness for them until they disperse. God will also remove the sorrow and answer the prayers of those who had come to ask'. 'Ali swore by the Lord of the Ka'aba that the *ahl al-bayt* and their friends had profitted both in this world and the next.

'*Surely God and His angels bless the Prophet. O you who believe! Call for blessings on him and salute him with a good salutation*' (33:56).

NOTES

1. Will Durant, *History of Western Civilization*, Vol. 1, pp.95, 301; Vol. 4, p.304; Vol. 7, p.95.

2. See the *Nahj ul-Balaghah* of Khuie, Vol. 2, p.173; *History of World Religions* (Persian translation), p.479.

3. The Persian translation of *Jahiliyat ul-qarn ul-'asharin* compiled by Muhammad Qutb.

4. *Nahj ul-Balaghah*, the first part printed in Damascus, p.66; *Fiyd ul-Islam*, Vol. 1, p.83, the 26th sermon.

5. The third edition of the Encyclopedia, p.255.

6. *Bihar ul-Anwar*, Vol. 15, p.325.

7. *Ibid.*, p.250.

8. *Kamil ul-Tawarikh*, second section, p.10; *Tabaqat*, Vol. L, p.61; *Bihar ul-Anwar*, Vol. 15, p.125.

9. *Bihar ul-Anwar*, Vol. 15, p.257.

10. *Ibid.*, pp.258-263.

11. *Ibid.*

12. *Sirihi Halabiyih*, Vol. 1, p.99.

13. *Bihar ul-Anwar*, Vol. 15, pp.331-395; *Sirihi ibn Hisham*, printed in 1375 A.H.L., Vol. l. pp.159-60; *Halabiyih*, printed in 1382 A.H.L., Vol. 1, p.99.

14. *Bihar ul-Anwar*, Vol. 15, pp.402, 406.

15. *Sirihi ibn Hisham*, Vol. 1, p.168.

16. *Bihar ul-Anwar*, Vol. 15, pp.382, 402, 366.

17. *Ibid*.

18. *Ibid*., p.336.

19. *Ibid*., p.142; *Sirihi ibn Hisham*, Vol. 1, p.168.

20. *Sirihi ibn Hisham*, Vol. 1, p.180.

21. Basra was a small town near Damascus.

22. Lat and Uzza were two of the famous idols that the Arabs worshipped and swore by on various occasions.

23. *Sirihi ibn Hisham*, Vol. 1, p.181; *A'lam Alwari*, published in Najaf, 1390 A.H.L., p.26; and *Bihar ul-Anwar*, Vol. 15, pp.193-204.

24. *Sirihi ibn Hisham*, Vol. 1, p.167 (footnote).

25. *Ibid*., p.183.

26. *Bihar ul-Anwar*, Vol. 16, p.3; *Tarikh Ya'aqubi*, Vol. 2, p.15.

27. *Ibid*., p.74.

28. *Bihar ul-Anwar*, Vol. 16, p.3; *Tarikh Ya'aqubi*, Vol. 2, p.15.

29. *A'yan ul-Shi'ah*, Vol. 2, p.8; *Sirihi Halabiyih*, Vol. 1, p.152.

30. *Sirihi ibn Hisham*, Vol. 1, p.188; *Bihar ul-Anwar*, Vol. 16, p.22.

31. *Bihar ul-Anwar*, Vol. 16, p.12; *Tarikh Tabari*, Vol. 3, p.1127.

32. *Sirihi ibn Hisham*, Vol. 1, p.188. This monk was not the monk who met the Prophet in his childhood.

33. *Kamil ibn Athir*, Vol. 2, p.39. Printed in Beirut, 1385 A.H.L.

34. *Bihar ul-Anwar*, Vol. 16, pp.20-21.

35. *Ibid*.

36. *Sirihi Halabiyih*, Vol. 1, p.152; *A'yan ul-Shi'ah*, Vol. 2, p.8.

37. *Bihar ul-Anwar*, Vol. 16, pp.56-73.

38. *Ibid.*, pp.7, 10; *A'lam Alwari*, p.146.

39. *Ibid.*, pp.10-71; *A'yan ul-Shi'ah*, Vol. 2, p.8.

40. *Ibid.*, p.3; *A'yan*, p.18; *A'lam*, p.146.

41. *Bihar ul-Anwar*, Vol. 16, pp.8, 13.

42. *Ibid.*

43. *Islam from the viewpoint of Voltaire*, second edition, p.5.

44. *Ibid.*, p.6.

45. *The Book of Samuel*, 2, section II.

46. *The Life of Muhammad*, compiled by Dr. Heykal, p.315.

47. *Muruj ul-Dhahab*, Vol. 2, p.287.

48. *Udhri Taqsir Bih Pishgahi Muhammad wa Qur'an*, p.35.

49. *Bihar ul-Anwar*, Vol. 22, pp.200-204.

50. *The Life of Muhammad*, compiled by Dr. Heykal, p.319.

51. *Ibid.*, p.320; *Bihar ul-Anwar*, Vol. 22, p.203.

52. *The Life of Muhammad*, compiled by Dr. Heykal, p.321.

53. *Bihar ul-Anwar*, Vol. 22, pp.214-218.

54. See *The Holy Qur'an*, Sura Ahzab, Ayah 37.

55. *Sirihi ibn Hisham*, Vol. 3, p.295.

56. *Isabih wa Isti'ab*, p.305; *Musu'ati Alenabi*, p.369; *Sirihi ibn Hisham*, Vol. 1, p.223; and *A'lam Alwari*, p.141.

57. *Ibid.*; *Musu'ati*, p.345, *A'lam*, p.142.

58. *Bihar ul-Anwar*, Vol. 22, p.203; *Sirihi ibn Hisham*, p.372; *Musu'ati Alenabi*, p.404.

59. *Rahbarani Buzurg va Masuliathayih Buzurgtar*, second edition, p.37.

60. Will Durant, Persian translation, Vol. 11, pp.1-10; *Al-Durrat ul-biyda fi Sharhi Khutbati Fatimati 'l-Zahra*, pp.27, 54.

61. *Da'irat ul-Ma'arif Farid Vajdi*, Vol. 6, p.250.

62. *Majma' ul-Bayan*, Vol. 10, p.534, new edition.

63. *Al-'Asr ul-Jahili*, Dr. Sufi Diyf, fifth edition in Egypt, p.70.

64. *Sharh ul-Mu'allaqat ul-Saba'a* by Alz-Zuzani, p.3.

65. *Bihar ul-Anwar*, Vol. 18, p.280.

66. *Ibid.*, pp.277-281; *Nahj ul-Balaghah* of Fiydul-Islam, p.802.

67. *A'lam Alwari*, pp.17-18; *Bihar ul-Anwar*, Vol. 15, p.410.

68. *Bihar ul-Anwar*, Vol. 16, p.224.

69. *Sirihi ibn Hisham*, Vol. 1, pp.192-197; *Bihar ul-Anwar*, Vol. 15, pp.337, 412.

70. *Bihar ul-Anwar*, Vol. 18, p.206.

71. *Manaqib*, Vol. 1, p.40

72. *Kamil*, Vol. 2, p.48; *Tarikhi Tabari*, Vol. 3, p.1148.

73. *Udhri Taqsir*, p.19.

74. *Ibid.*, p.18.

75. Hysteria is a mental disease.

76. *Udhri Taqsir*, p.20.

77. *Sirihi ibn Hisham*, Vol. 1, p.237.

78. *The Life of Muhammad*, compiled by Dr. Heykal, p.134.

79. *A'lam Alwari*, p.47.

80. *Sirihi ibn Hisham*, Vol. 1, p.238.

81. *Manaqib*, Vol. 1, p.42.

82. *Sirihi ibn Hisham*, Vol. 1, p.246; *Bihar ul-Anwar*, Vol. 18, p.208.

83. *Ibid.*, *Sirihi*, p.245; *Bihar*, p.188; *Al-Ghadir*, Vol. 3, pp.219-241; *Tarikhi Tabari*, Vol. 3, p.1160.

84. *Wasa'il ul-Shi'a*, second edition, 1384 A.H.L., Vol. 3, pp.16, 17.

85. *Ibid.*

86. *A'lam Alwari*, p.37; *Jami' ul-Ahadithi Shi'a*, Vol. 2, p.31. It is to be noted that at that time each of the prayers was two cycles (*rak'at*).

87. *Tarikhi Tabari,* Vol. 3, p.1122.

88. *A'lam Alwari,* p.38, printed in 1390; *Tarikhi Tabari,* Vol. 3, p.1162.

89. *Tarikhi Tabari,* Vol. 3, pp.1171-1173; *Tafsiri Majma' ul-Bayan,* Vol. 7, p.206; *Bihar ul-Anwar,* Vol. 18, p.192. This point is confirmed by all Islamic as well as non-Islamic historians and is among the confirmed facts of history. *Al-Ghadir,* Vol. 2, p.278.

90. *Tarikhi Ya'qubi,* Vol. 2, p.22.

91. *Sirihi ibn Hisham,* Vol. 1, p.262; *Tarikhi Ya'qubi,* Vol. 2, p.19.

92. This phrase was used by the Arabs whenever they wanted to draw the attention of the people to an important issue.

93. *Tarikhi Tabari,* Vol. 3, p.1170.

94. *Sirihi Halabiyih,* Vol. 1, p.311.

95. *Tarikhi Tabari,* Vol. 3, p.1170; *Manaqib,* Vol.1, pp.43-44.

96. *Sirihi ibn Hisham,* Vol. 1, pp.265-266.

97. *Ibid.,* pp.266-267.

98. *Sirihi ibn Hisham,* Vol. 1, pp.295-1296.

99. *Tarikhi Tabari,* Vol. 3, p.1176.

100. *A'lam Alwari,* new edition, p.57.

101. *Manaqib* Vol. 1, p.51.

102. *A'lam Alwari,* p.58.

103. *Kamil,* Vol. 2, pp.66-67.

104. *Ibid.*

105. *Ibid.,* p.108.

106. *A'lam Alwari,* pp.55-61.

107. *Tarikhi Tabari,* Vol. 3, p.1229; *A'lam Alwari,* pp.61-62.

108. *Tarikhi Tabari,* Vol. 3, p.1231; *Bihar ul-Anwar,* Vol. 19, p.60.

109. *Sirihi ibn Hishim,* Vol. 1; p.481; *Tarikhi Tabari,* Vol. 3, p.1232.

110. *Bihar ul-Anwar, Vol. 19, p.78.*

111. *Tarikhi Tabari,* Vol. 3, p.1234.

112. *A'lam Alwari*, p.63.

113. *Sirihi ibn Hisham*, Vol. 1, p.486; *Bihar ul-Anwar*, Vol. 19, p.69.

114. *Ibid.*, p.489; p.88.

115. *Kamil*, p.106. Quba is a place near Medina.

116. *Tarikhi Tabari*, Vol. 3, p.1245.

117. *Bihar ul-Anwar*, Vol. 19, p.116.

118. *Kamil*, Vol. 2, p.106.

119. *Sirihi ibn Hisham*, Vol. 1, p.494; *Bihar ul-Anwar*, Vol. 9, p.122.

120. *Mu'jim ul-Buldan maddihi Yathrib* and *Majma' ul-Bahrin Maddihi Tharb*.

121. *Bihar ul-Anwar*, Vol. 73, p.293; *Rudih Kafi*, p.246.

122. *Sirihi ibn Hisham*, Vol. 2, pp.504-505.

123. *Usul ul-Kafi*, Vol. 2, pp.166-167.

124. *Ibid.*, p.169.

125. *A'lam Alwari*, p.69.

126. *Tarikhi Tabari*, Vol. 5, p.2271.

127. *Bihar ul-Anwar*, Vol. 20, p.350.

128. *Ibid.*, p.362.

129. *A'lam Alwari*, p.110.

130. *Kamil*, Vol. 2, pp.248-249.

131. *Usud ul-Ghabih*, Vol. 1, p.206.

132. *Tamadduni Islam wa Arab*, p.807.

133. *Jang wa sulh dar Islam*, translated by Sayyid Ghulam Riza Sa'idi, p.345.

134. *Bihar ul-Anwar*, Vol. 19, p.143.

135. *Muhammad sitari kih dar maccih dirrakhshid*, p.92.

136. *Bihar ul-Anwar*, Vol. 19, pp.265-266.

137. *Kamil*, Vol. 2, p.118; *A'lam Alwari*, p.76.

138. *Tabaqat*, pp.27-29.

139. *Tarikhi Tabari*, Vol. 3, pp.1463-1476.

140. A Jewish tribe residing near Medina.

141. *Bihar ul-Anwar*, Vol. 20, p.191; *Tarikhi Tabari*, Vol. 3, p.1472.

142. *Tarikhi Tabari*, Vol. 3, pp.1487-1493.

143. *Kamil*, Vol. 2, p.192; *Tarikhi Tabari*, Vol. 3, p.1511.

144. *Kamil*, Vol. 2, p.216; *Tabaqat*, Vol. 2, pp.77-78; *Tarikhi Tabari*, Vol. 3, pp.1575-1584.

145. A place near Damascus.

146. *Tabaqat*, Vol. 2, pp.92-94.

147. *A'lam Alwari*, pp.104-112; *Bihar ul-Anwar*, Vol. 21, p.106.

148. *Kamil*, Vol. 2, pp.247-250.

149. *Bihar ul-Anwar*, Vol. 21, p.149.

150. *Sirihi ibn Hisham*, p.482.

151. *Tamaddun*, p.148.

152. *Kamil*, Vol. 2, p.61.

153. *Safinat ul-Bihar*, Vol. 2, p.413.

154. *Kamil*, Vol. 2, p.210; *Makatib ul-Rasul*, Vol. 1, pp.30-31.

155. *Makatib ul-Rasul*, Vol. 1, pp.35-41, 60-182.

156. *Ibid.*, p.90; *Sirihi Halabiyih*, Vol. 3, p.277.

157. *Muhammad wa zamamdaran*, p.162.

158. *Sirihi Halabiyih*, Vol. 3, p.285.

159. *Makatib ul-Rasul*, Vol. 1, p.172.

160. *Al-bidayah wal Nahayah*, Vol. 5, p.53.

161. *Bihar ul-Anwar*, Vol. 21, p.361.

162. The law of emergency is applied in emergency situations. The law of non-guilt is applied in cases of severe trouble. The law of no loss is applied when a loss may occur. The conditions and qualifications of these laws have been explained in detail in the books on theology and jurisprudence.

163. *Jami' ul-Javami'*, p.275; *Tafsir al-Mizan*, Vol. 2, p.144; *Tafsir ul-Kashif*, Vol. 3, p.164; *Tafsir ul-Biyadwi*, p.477; *al-Bayan*, Vol. 7, p.91; *Ruh ul-Ma'ani*, Vol. 22, p.32.

164. *Mustadrak*, Vol. 2, p.262.

165. *Usul ul-Kafi*, Vol. 1, p.177.

166. *Najh ul-Balaghah*, Fiyd ul-Islam, sermonn 133, p.403.

167. *Kamil*, Vol. 2, p. 278.

168. *Uyun akhbar ul-Reza*, Vol. 2, p.80.

169. Encyclopedia of *Farid Vadji*, Vol. 3, p.542.

170. *Al-Ghadir*, Vol. 1, p.9.

171. *Kamil*, pol.p.216, 278, 242.

172. *Tarikhi Tabari*, Vol. 3, pp.1171-1173.

173. *Fadail ul-Khamsih*, printed by Dar ul-Khutub ul-Islamiyah, Vol. 1, pp.178-186.

174. *Al-Ghadir*, Vol. 1, pp.9-11.

175. *Ibid.*, pp.60-61.

176. *Al-Ghadir*, Vol. 1, pp.166-174.

177. *Ibid.*, pp.198-199.

178. *Ibid.*, pp.14-61.

179. Twenty-six have been mentioned in the first volume of *Al-Ghadir*, pp.152-157.

180. *Al-Ghadir*, Vol. 2, pp.34-41.

181. *Ibid.*, Vol. 1, pp.270-271.

182. *Ibid.*, pp.274.

183. *Bihar ul-Anwar*, Vol. 16, pp.220-229.

184. *Ibid.*

185. *Kohl ul-basar*, p.69.

186. *Bihar ul-Anwar*, Vol. 16, pp.226-228.

187. *Ibid.*, p.240.

188. *Ibid.*, pp.229, 281, 182.

189. *Kohl*, pp.67-68.

190. *Bihar ul-Anwar*, Vol. 16, pp.226-232.

191. *Kohl*, pp.67-68.

192. *Bihar ul-Anwar*, Vol. 16, pp.228-229.

193. *Ibid.*, pp.264-265.

194. *Kamil*, Vol. 2, p.252.

195. *Ibid.*, pp.248-252.

196. *Irshad us-Sari Lisharhi Sahih Bukhari*, Vol. 9, p.456.

197. *Wasa'il*, new edition, Vol. 1, p.442.

198. *Ibid.*, Vol. 1, p.443.

199. *Safinat*, Vol. 1, p.419.

200. *Wasa'il*, new edition, Vol. 1, p.349.

201. *Ibid.*, Vol. 16, p.472.

202. *Ibid.*, Vol. 3, p.344.

203. *Ibid.*, Vol. 1, p.365.

204. *Kohl*, p.78.

Index

A

Aaron, 113
'Abbas, 58
'Abdullah, 20-22, 26, 58
'Abdullah ibn Rawahah, 97
Abdul Dar, 46
Abdul Muttalib, 21-23, 25, 26, 40, 58, 59
Abraham, the Prophet, 46, 115
Abu Amayah, 46
Abu Bakr, 77, 78, 119
Abu Halah, 32
Abu Jahl, 67, 70, 72, 91, 95
Abu Lahab, 59, 64, 70, 71
Abu Sufyan, 41, 42, 70, 127
Abu Talib, 22, 23, 25-27, 57, 58, 65-67, 117, 119
Abwa, 22
Adam, the Prophet, 27

Africa, 85
Ahad, 72
Ahl al-Bayt, 130
Ahmad, 29
Ahzab (Trench), the war of, 96, 99
'Aisha, 39, 41
'Akaz, 26
Akramah ibn Abu Jahl, 98
Ali, Imam, 16, 57-60, 77, 78, 82, 96, 107, 113, 117, 118, 129
  succession of, 115-121
Allah, 15-17, 22, 23, 27, 31, 40, 45, 46, 49, 52-60, 63, 65-67, 71, 72, 77, 80-84, 87-91, 93-98, 101-107, 111, 114-121, 124-130
        attributes of, 31, 32, 50, 109, 112
        the Creator, 51, 52, 55, 58, 102, 128
Amina, 19-22
'Ammar, 45
'Ammar Yasir, 71, 72
'Ammarat ibn Walid, 66
Amr ul-Qays, 44
Anas ibn Malik, 126
Angel of Revelation *see* Gabriel
'Anizah, 44
Ansar, 119
Anushiravan, 20
Apostle *see* Muhammad, the Prophet (upon whom be peace)
'Aqibah ibn Abi Ma'ayyat, 70
Arabs, the, 15, 16, 21, 41, 44, 60, 63, 66, 89, 103, 125
Arabia, 14, 32, 44, 57, 58, 103, 124
 before Islam, 14-17, 44, 45
'As ibn Wa'il, 70
Asamata ibn Zayd, 127
Asia, 85
Aswad ibn Abd Yaghwan, 70
'Atif, 58
Atigh Makhzumi, 32
Aws, 76, 96
ayat-i-tathir, 129

B

Badr, the war of, 94, 95, 99

Bahira, 26, 27, 55, 56
Bani Bakr, 97
Bani Hashim, 119
Bani Israel, 42
Bani Mustalaq, 41
 war of the, 96, 97, 99
Bani Nazir, 42, 96
Bani Qurayzah, the war of, 96, 99
Bani Sa'd, 21
Bani Ummayad, 42
Baqir, Imam, 113
Basra, 26, 97
Bible, the, 50
Bilal, 72, 83, 91
Black Stone, the, 46, 47
Book, the Holy see Qur'an, the

C

Caliph, 60, 119, 121
caliphate, 116-118, 120, 121
Christ *see* Jesus
Christians, the, 13, 37, 38, 41, 51, 55, 56, 88, 92, 94, 99
Christianity, 13, 53
churches, 94, 95
colonialists, 101, 123
Creator *see* Allah
crusades, 94, 99

D

Damascus, 20, 26, 33, 56
Davenport, John, 39, 52
Day of Judgment (Resurrection), 57, 114

E

Ethiopia, 40, 41, 72, 83, 91

F

Fakh pasturage, 45
Fatima, 34, 128-130
Fatima Makhzumiyah, 127

G

Gabriel, 50, 52, 55-57, 117, 130
Ghadir Khum, 115-121
God *see* Allah
God's House *see Ka'aba, also Masjid ul-Haram*

H

Hafsa, 39, 41
Hajj, 76, 115, 117
hajjis, 115, 119
Halima, 21
Harith, 21, 41
Harith ibn 'Umar, 97
Harqal, King, 105
Hasan, Imam, 129
Havazin, 98
Hawzah, 105
Hayy ibn Akhtab, 42
Hijaz, the, 19, 28, 103, 115, 117, 118
hijra, 75-80, 88, 95, 96
 beginning of, 79, 80
Hind, 127

Hissan ibn Sabit, 121
Hudaybiyah, 90, 97
Hunayn, the battle of, 90, 98, 99
Husayn, Imam, 119, 129

I

Ibn Athir, 71
Ibn Hisham, 41
Imamate, 121
Imams, 112, 121
Iran, 104
Islam, 13, 22, 31, 34, 38-41, 44, 46, 47, 49-61, 63-67, 69-73, 75-80, 83-85, 87-99, 101-107, 113, 116-121, 124-130
  advent of, 49-52, 55-57, 79, 91, 103, 104
  enemies of, 37, 38, 41, 42, 58, 65, 69-73, 75-78, 90, 91, 95
  propagation of, 57-61, 63-72, 79, 83, 98, 101-107, 124
  universality of, 104, 110-112
  world before the advent of, 13-17
Islamic brotherhood, 81-85, 87
Islamic government, 89, 97

J

Ja'far ibn Abi Talib, 97
Ja'far al-Sadiq, Imam *see* Sadiq, Imam Ja'far al-
Jahash, 40
Jeddah, 90
Jesus Christ, 94
Jews, the, 13, 22, 23, 27, 56, 88, 97, 105, 106
Jihad, 87-99, 111
  purpose of, 88-99
John Andre Maure, 37
Jawayriya, 39, 41

K

Ka'aba, 15, 23, 44, 46, 49, 58, 76, 98, 115, 130
  dispute over the, 46, 47
  pilgrimage to the, 76, 97, 98, 115
Khadija, 29, 32-35, 38, 40, 45, 56-58
  marriage of the Prophet to, 34, 35
Khalid ibn Walid, 98
khatam, 113
Khaybar, the war of, 97, 99
Khaza'ah, 96, 97
Khazraj, 76
Khusrow, King, 104
Khuwalid, 32, 58
Khuzayma, 40

L

Labayka, 115
Lat, 26
Lord *see* Allah

M

magi, 105
Majnah, 26
Makkah, 13, 19, 22, 26, 28, 65, 75-79, 90, 94-99, 115
  advent of Islam in, 103, 104
  conquest of, 90, 97, 127
  migration of the Prophet from, 76-80, 94, 103
  suffering of Muslims in, 69-73, 94, 95, 98
Mana, 58, 119
Maris'a, 97
Marqal, 97

Marya, 39
Mas'ab ibn 'Umir, 76
Masara, 32, 33, 56
Masjid ul-Haram, 58, 76, 97, 116
mawla, 120, 121
Maymuna, 39, 41
Medina, 20, 22, 79, 82, 88, 90, 95-98, 116
 arrival of the Prophet in, 79
 establishment of Islam in, 79, 81-85
 migration to, 75-80, 88, 94, 103
Medinat ul-Nabi, 79
Messenger, the *see* Muhammad, the Prophet
Middle Ages, 37
monotheism, 57, 58, 63, 71, 75, 103, 115
Moses, the Prophet, 13, 56, 105, 106, 113
mosques, 46, 82, 95
Mount Hira, 45, 50, 55
Mount Safa, 63, 64
Mount Sinai, 106
Muhammad, the Prophet (peace and the mercy of God be upon him and his descendants), 15, 22, 25-27, 29, 32, 37, 38, 40, 46, 50, 52, 56, 58, 78, 91, 104-106, 112-114, 124
 as a blessing to the world, 87, 103
 birth and childhood of, 19-29
 character of, 22, 23, 98, 123-130
  before the prophetic mission, 43-47
 hardships suffered by, 69-73, 94, 98, 127
 the last Prophet, 109-114
 marriages of, 31, 37-42
 migration of, 75-80, 94, 103
 prophetic mission of, 50-130
 sayings of, 112
 the Trustworthy one, 45, 46
 wars of the, 93-99
  motives for the, 94-99
Mu'awiyah, 119
Muquqs, 104
Musa ibn 'Imran, 105
Mutah, the war of, 97, 99

N

Nabi, 113
Nafisa, 34
Nahj al-Balaghah, 16
Najashi, 104
Najran, Bishop, 106
nationalism, 15
New Testament, 50, 51

O

Old Testament, 50, 51

P

paganism, 58
Persia, 20, 83, 104
pilgrimage, 97, 115
prayers, ritual, 57, 58, 118, 126, 128, 129
prophecy, 75, 104, 109, 112, 125
prophets, 52, 55, 56, 63, 94, 102, 113, 124

Q

Qasim, 34
Quba, 78
Qur'an, the, 38, 51, 75, 77, 82, 83, 88, 93, 104, 112, 113, 118, 124, 129
Quraysh, the, 23, 26, 27, 29, 32-34, 40, 46, 47, 64-73, 76-79, 81, 90, 94-97, 103, 117, 127

R

Rabi ul-Awwal, 20, 78
Red Sea, 95
Revelation, 50, 52-54, 67, 118
 beginning of, 49, 52
 end of, 112-114
Riza, Imam, 114
Rome, 97, 105
Ruqiyah, 34
Rustam Farrokhzad, 89

S

Sa'ad Ma'az, 96
Sadiq, Imam Ja'far al-, 82, 83, 103
Safia, 39, 41, 42
Safwan ibn Umayyah, 90
Saghif, 98
Salman (the Persian), 83
Saraqa ibn Malik, 78
Sauda bint Zama, 39, 40
Savah Lake, 21
Shaybah, 70
Sumayyah, 72
Sura Yasin, 77
synagogues, 95

T

Tahir, 34
Ta'if, 90, 98, 99
Tariq Maharibi, 71
Thawr Cave, 77, 78
Tradition of the Cloak, 129
Trinity, the, 14

U

Uhud, the war of, 95, 99
'Umar, 119
Ummah, 56, 116, 119, 120
Umm Habiba, 39, 41
Umm Kulsum, 34
Umm Salma, 39, 40
'Utbah, 70
'Uzza, 26

V

Vajdi, Farid, 115
vali, 120

W

Walid, 46
Walid ibn Maghirah, 70
Warqa ibn Nawfal, 33, 56

Y

Yamamah, 105
Yasir, 72
Yathrib, 26, 76

Z

zakat, 84, 129
Zayd ibn Harith, 40, 97
Zaynab, 34
Zaynab bint Jahash, 39-41
Zaynab bint Khuzayma, 39, 40
Zil-Majaz, 26